MIDI BASICS

by Akira Otsuka & Akihiko Nakajima.

All the essential facts about MIDI contained in one easy-to-read book.

MIDI BASICS

by Akira Otsuka & Akihiko Nakajima.

Amsco Publications
London/New York/Sydney/Cologne

Exclusive Distributors:
Music Sales Limited
8/9 Frith Street, London W1V 5TZ, England.
Music Sales Pty. Limited
27 Clarendon Street, Artarmon, Sydney, NSW 2064, Australia.
Music Sales Corporation
24 East 22nd Street, New York, NY 10010, USA.

Translation by Takako Imai and Nick Wood.
Editorial Consultant Vince Hill.
Translation arranged by Rittor Music Europe Limited.

Cover design by Mike Bell.
Book design by Paul Higgins.
Cover illustration by Plum Illustration.
Typesetting by Capital Setters & Type Gallery.

© Copyright Rittor Music Inc. Tokyo, Japan.
This edition © Copyright 1987 Amsco Publications.

USA ISBN 0.8256.1091.5
UK ISBN 0.7119.0952.0
Order No. AM63447

Music Sales complete catalogue lists thousands of titles and is free from
your local music book shop, or direct from Music Sales Limited.
Please send 50p in stamps for postage to
Music Sales Limited, 8/9 Frith Street, London W1V 5TZ.

Unauthorised reproduction of any part of
this publication by any means including photocopying
is an infringement of copyright.

Printed in England by
The Anchor Press Limited, Tiptree, Essex.

CONTENTS

(1) THE WORLD OF MIDI... 4
All You Need Is A Single Cable... 4
MIDI Column 1 – DIN MIDI Cable... 5
Connection Of MIDI Terminals 6
MIDI Is For Complete Systems... 10
MIDI Channels... 10
MIDI Column 2 – The 4 MIDI Modes....................................... 14
Channel Information 14
System Information 19

(2) MIDI IN PRACTICE... 20
Hardware 23, 27, 30, 34, 37, 40, 42, 45, 47, 50
Implementation Chart 54
Index 58
MIDI Column 3 – Rhythm Machine/Sequencer Synchronisation 43
MIDI Specifications: Description 56
Software: Aftertouch, How To Use It Depends On Your Instrument .. 39
Software: Channel And Mode, The Basic Transmit/Receive
    Condition 36
Software: Control Change, The Organisation of Controllers 44
Software: The MIDI Cable, Its Structure And Length 25
Software: The MIDI Message, Requires Only A Single Cable........... 28
Software: The MIDI Terminal, Connecting Instruments................. 21
Software: Note On/Note Off, The Most Basic MIDI Message 32
Software: The Pitch Wheel, Why It Has Its Own MIDI Message........ 46
Software: Program Change, Achieving It On Various Synthesisers...... 41
Software: System Messages, Information Used By The Whole
    System.. 48

① THE WORLD OF MIDI

The word MIDI is used more and more frequently in the world of music but many people do not yet understand its true meaning, use and significance. Words such as RGB and Twin-Cam may seem very glamorous but real knowledge of these inventions is known only to a few experts. Technology can advance so rapidly that sometimes we may barely acknowledge the existence, let alone the function of new equipment or inventions, before they are superseded. To enjoy watching colour television you don't have to understand RGB, but for the modern musician a deep understanding of MIDI is becoming a vital element in music creation.

Nearly all modern keyboards include a MIDI function and it is generally agreed that this standard is brilliant. Music magazines often include articles on MIDI or use the word MIDI in their articles but these explanations can be difficult to follow and you may only grasp the idea that the use of computers seems to be effective in creating music.

So, What Is MIDI? and what are its advantages? This easy to read booklet serves as a practical guide to MIDI for both the beginner and the more advanced user.

ALL YOU NEED IS A SINGLE CABLE

In live performance how can one musician play synthesiser and piano in perfect unison? Through long practice of classical piano scales you may be able to play the synthesiser with your left hand and the piano with your right hand.

But even if you are a good player it may seem almost impossible to play different instruments simultaneously and in perfect unison. Anyway, many people hate practising classical scales and this is not a route they may wish to follow. A good player with the correct technique has the capacity to play two keyboards, but if you have to play the same phrase with electric piano, synthesiser and strings at the same time it is impossible for one person. In the recording studio multi-track recorders can be used to endlessly overdub sound, while in live performance two keyboards are the limit of sound creation for one person, three if you use a footpedal.

Using MIDI these limitations are easily overcome. Any MIDI keyboard can act as a Master to control one or more other keyboards – (Slaves) – connected via the MIDI sockets on each instrument. As MIDI is a standard that has been agreed among all

MIDI BASICS

manufacturers producing MIDI instruments, the master and slave instruments do not all have to be the product of a single manufacturer e.g. a Yamaha DX7 master can control a Roland JX-10 slave (and vice-versa).

So how do we connect these instruments? The familiar jack-to-jack or phono-to-phono cables are not suitable for MIDI connections, instead 180 degree 5-pin DIN-to-DIN cable is used. You can make your own or buy ready-made cables from any musical instrument dealer. A maximum length of 15 metres is recommended, as longer lengths may cause the signal to deteriorate.

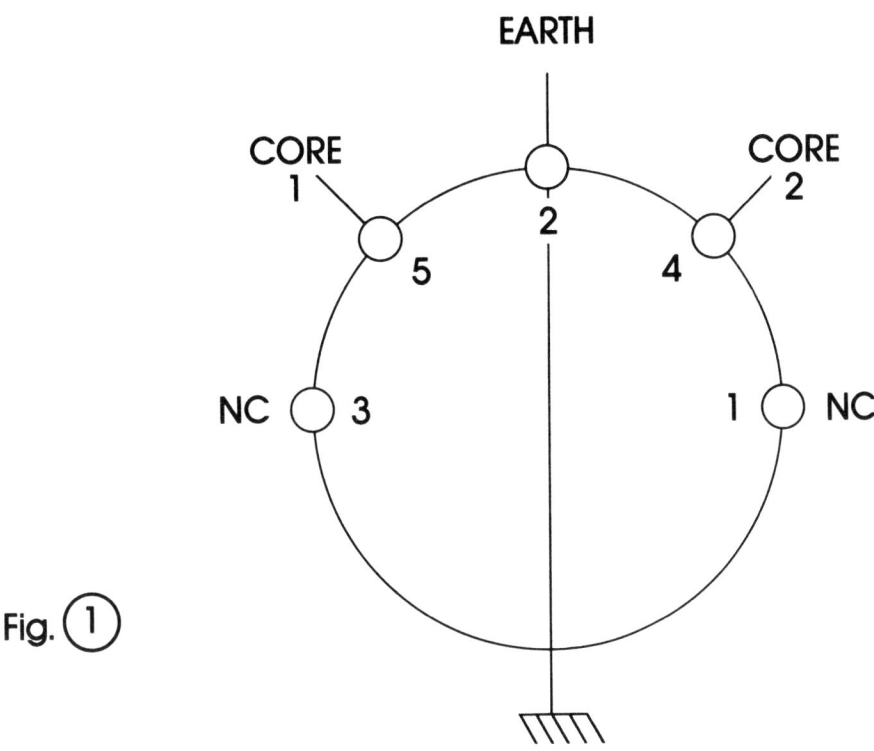

Fig. 1

MIDI COLUMN 1 – DIN MIDI CABLE

You might think that as each MIDI connector is a 5-pin DIN plug that the cable used to carry the MIDI signal would require 5 (or 6 with earth) strands. But the MIDI signal is in fact carried by only 3 strands including earth. Hence you can make up MIDI cable from standard 2-core shielded microphone cable.

5-pin DIN is a European standard and the pins are numbered as shown in Fig.1 with only pins 4,2 and 5 being used. Pin 2 is connected to the metal shielding of the plug which acts as the earth. The cable shielding is soldered to this flange and the core leads are soldered to pins 4 and 5. Attention must be paid to the soldering, particularly of pins 4 and 5.

Doing it yourself is a lot cheaper than buying readymade MIDI cables, just be certain that pins 4 and 5 are not crossed.

CONNECTION OF MIDI TERMINALS

If you look at the sockets on your MIDI instrument you will find 2 or 3 terminals (occasionally only 1), marked MIDI IN, MIDI OUT and MIDI THRU. All these terminals are 180 degree 5-pin DIN.

Fig. (2)　　▲ MIDI TERMINALS

In a Master-Slave instrument combination the MIDI cable is connected between the master MIDI OUT and the slave MIDI IN terminals. The MIDI signal is transmitted from the OUT terminal and received at the IN terminal. With the two instruments connected in this manner playing in perfect unison is now a practical proposition, for example as in the case previously mentioned of an electric piano and a synthesiser. If the piano is used as the master instrument then the synthesiser can be controlled as a slave. As well as the instrument to instrument MIDI connection, if you require both instruments to be heard each has to be connected (e.g. with jack-to-jack cable) to some form of monitoring system (i.e. an

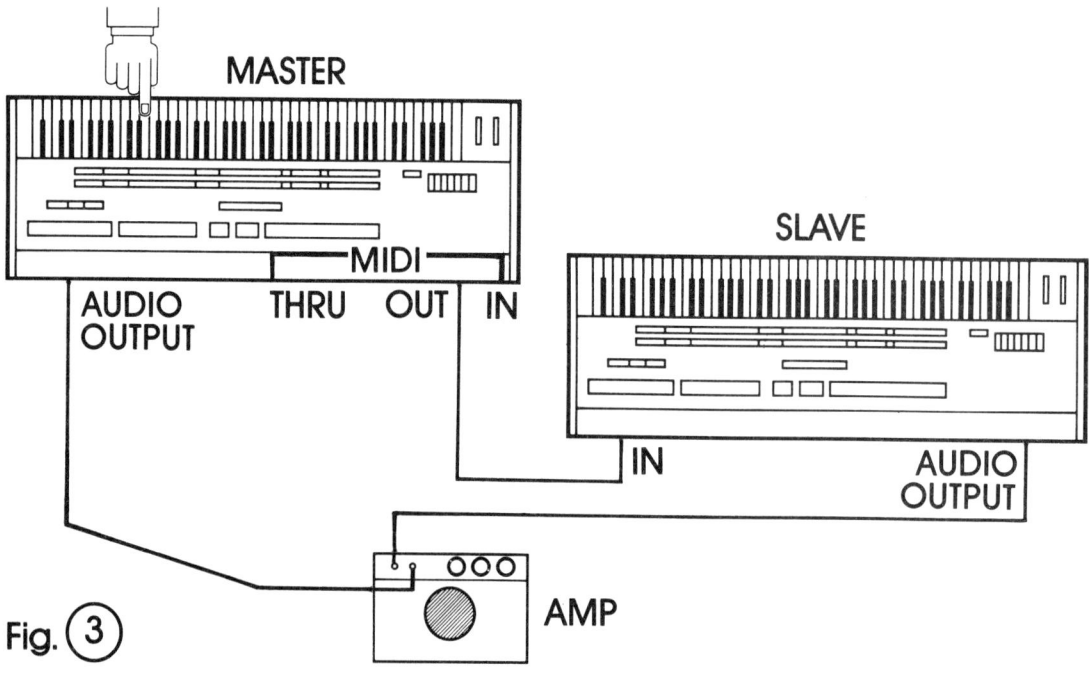

Fig. (3)

amplifier or mixer/MTR). It is important to realise that the MIDI signal and the signal that carries the audio output of the instrument are completely different types of electrical information. MIDI cables should never be connected to anything other than MIDI terminals.

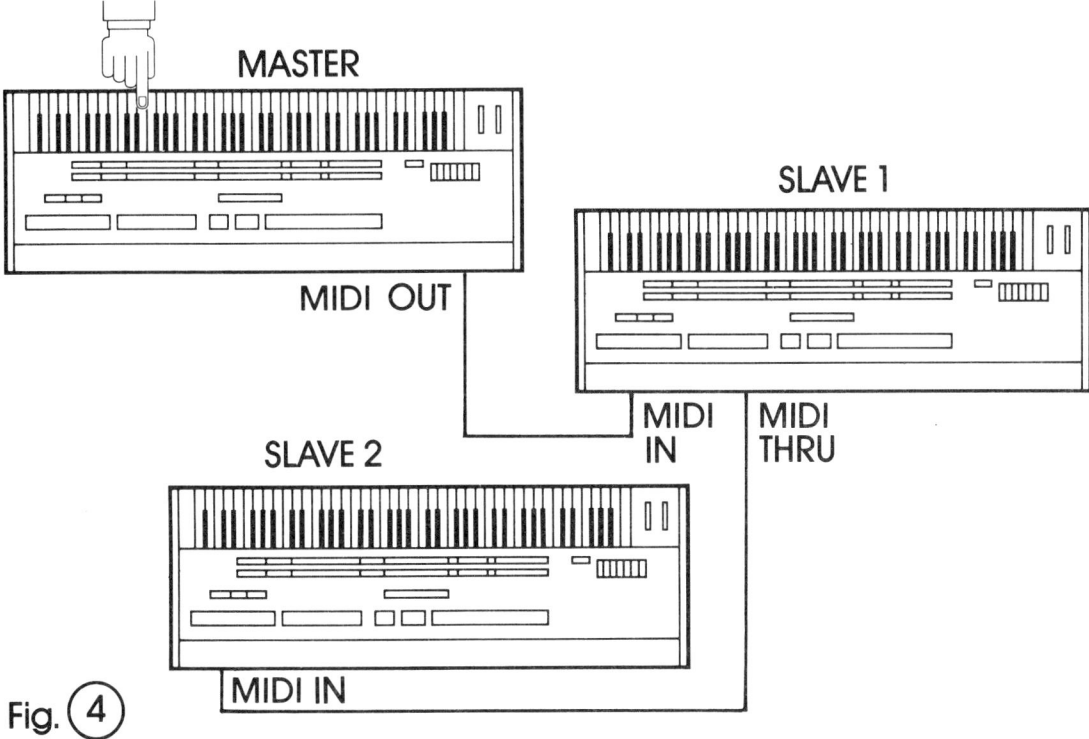

Fig. 4

So how do we connect more than two instruments? If the slave has a MIDI THRU terminal then this is easily accomplished (see fig.4). A MIDI connection is made from the MIDI THRU terminal on the first slave to the MIDI IN terminal on the second slave. You might think that this process of 'daisy chaining' instruments together could continue, limited only by your bank balance, but in practice with more than a few instruments you start to encounter MIDI delay. Even with only two or three slaves this can be a problem, especially if the music you are playing is up tempo. Each slave receives the MIDI signal in turn and the further from the master instrument the slave is, the later it receives its MIDI commands.

When using MIDI THRU you should remember that the MIDI THRU terminal sends out exactly the same MIDI commands that the MIDI IN terminal receives. You might think that these two terminals are simply wired in parallel, but this is not in fact the case, simple circuitry exists between the IN and THRU terminals which acts as a buffer and amplifies the signal before sending it out through the THRU terminal. It is this process which causes the MIDI delay. With only one slave instrument this delay is not too significant, but with the addition of further instruments the effect accumulates as the MIDI signal encounters each THRU terminal.

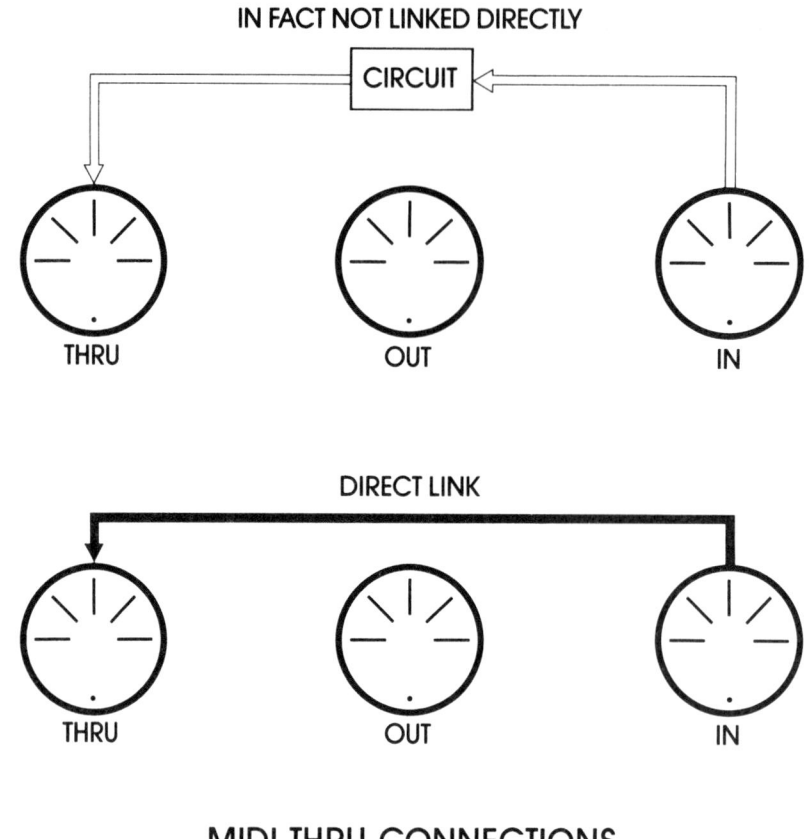

Fig. (5)   MIDI THRU CONNECTIONS

So how can we solve this problem of MIDI delay? What is really needed is a MIDI expansion box. This is based on the same idea as using an expansion box for sending instrument audio output to several destinations e.g. adding additional amplifiers/mixers/MTR etc. to a single keyboard (see fig.6). Just as this takes a single audio signal and distributes it to various sources so a MIDI expansion box does the same with the MIDI signal.

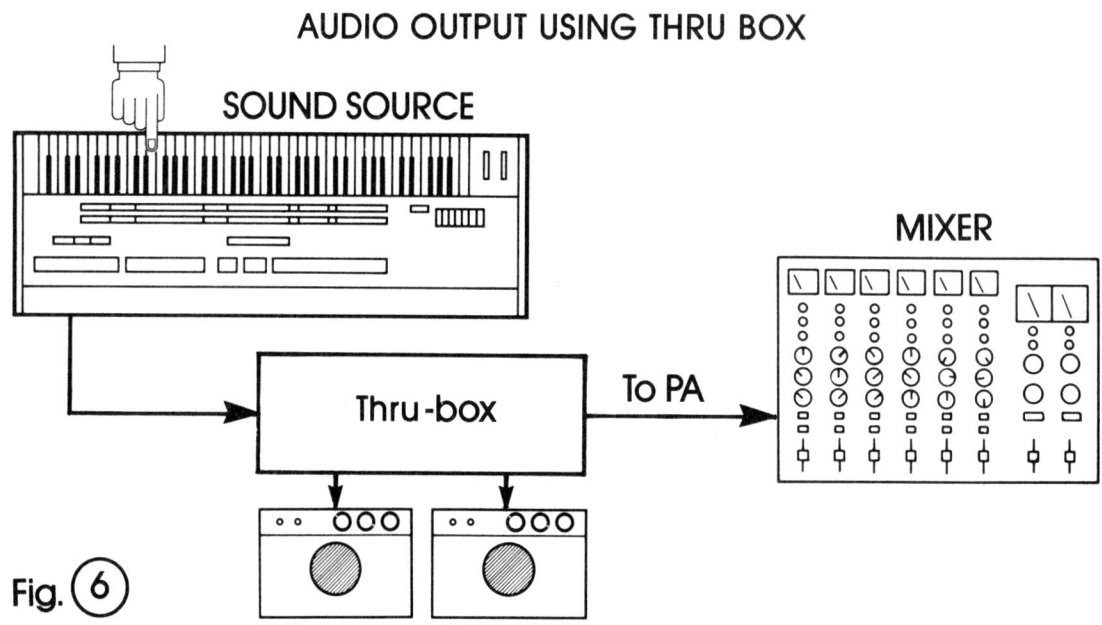

Fig. (6)

MIDI BASICS

MIDI THRU BOXES

▲ YAMAHA YME 8

▲ ROLAND MM-4

Fig.

This type of MIDI Expansion/THRU Box bears a different name according to the manufacturer, e.g. Yamaha – MIDI EXPANDER or Roland – MIDI THRU BOX (see fig.7). The configuration of MIDI IN and MIDI THRU terminals varies with different models. Those most commonly used are 1 IN-4 OUT, 2 IN-4 OUT and 4 IN-8 OUT.

So in practice the MIDI OUT of the master instrument is connected to a MIDI IN terminal on the expansion box. Each MIDI THRU terminal on the box can now be connected to the MIDI IN of a separate slave instrument, enabling the master instrument to control several slaves without the problem of MIDI signal delay. Also, if your slave instrument has no MIDI THRU and you want to control another slave, a MIDI expansion box is essential.

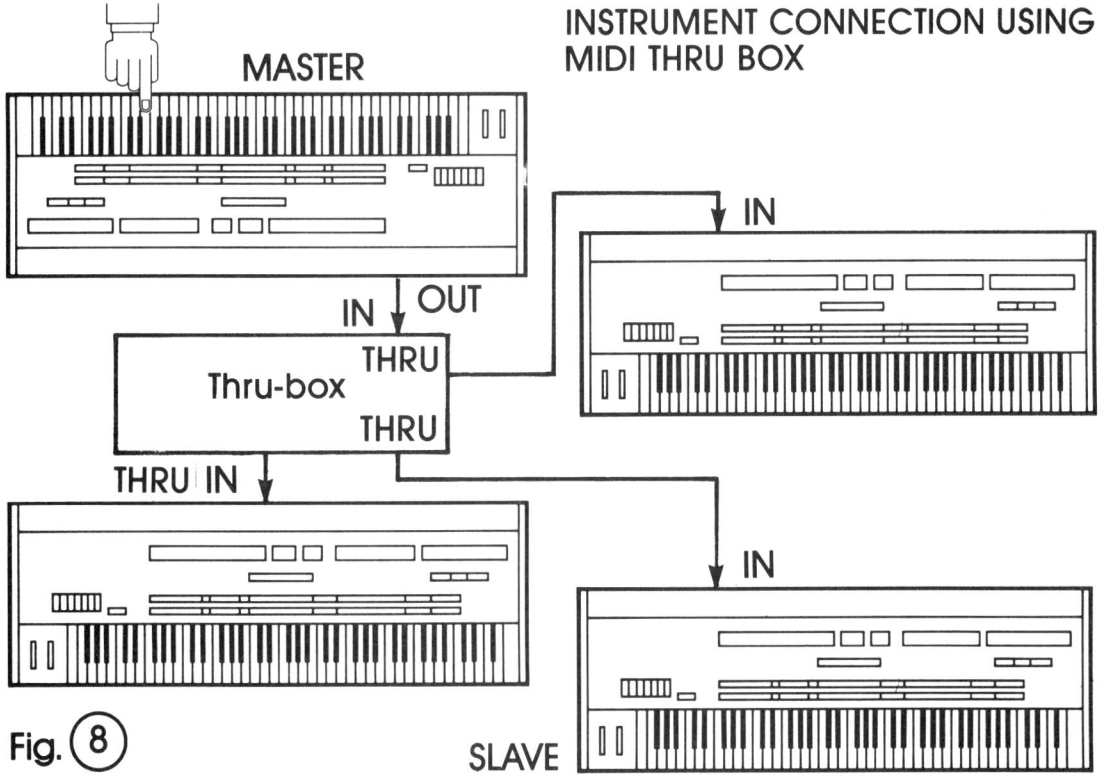

INSTRUMENT CONNECTION USING MIDI THRU BOX

Fig. 8

MIDI IS FOR COMPLETE SYSTEMS

By now you will have realised that MIDI facilitates the interconnection of musical instruments. It is also possible to connect your instruments to effects units, sequencers and computers if they have suitable MIDI connections. so we see that the essence of MIDI lies in the creation of complete MIDI systems. The minimum requirement to create such a system and hence make use of MIDI is two pieces of MIDI equipment. However, even if you only have a single MIDI keyboard it is still useful to know about MIDI, especially for live performance, as increasingly MIDI facilities are being applied to instruments which can always be hired, borrowed or begged as the situation demands. In this way your sound can be enriched enormously and if you don't understand how to apply MIDI, when the time comes opportunities will be missed. Also, when working in the studio or playing live, knowledge of MIDI will enable you to produce the sounds you desire more easily and effectively.

MIDI CHANNELS

We have seen so far how MIDI enables a master keyboard to control many slaves, in the sense that whatever is played on the master is simultaneously played on the slave instruments. As well as this MIDI makes it possible for you to change the voice of the slave from the master as well as manipulating various controllers if they are accessible via MIDI. If your master/slave are identical machines or have identical voice programming then you can also exchange voice data. How then are these various MIDI functions applied in practice?

NORMAL TRANSMISSION DATA

DATA	CONTENT
NOTE ON	No. OF KEY PRESSED
NOTE OFF	No. OF KEY RELEASED
SUSTAIN SWITCH	SWITCH ON/OFF
PITCH BENDER	DIRECTION/QUANTITY
VELOCITY*	STRENGTH OF KEY PRESSED

Fig. (9)

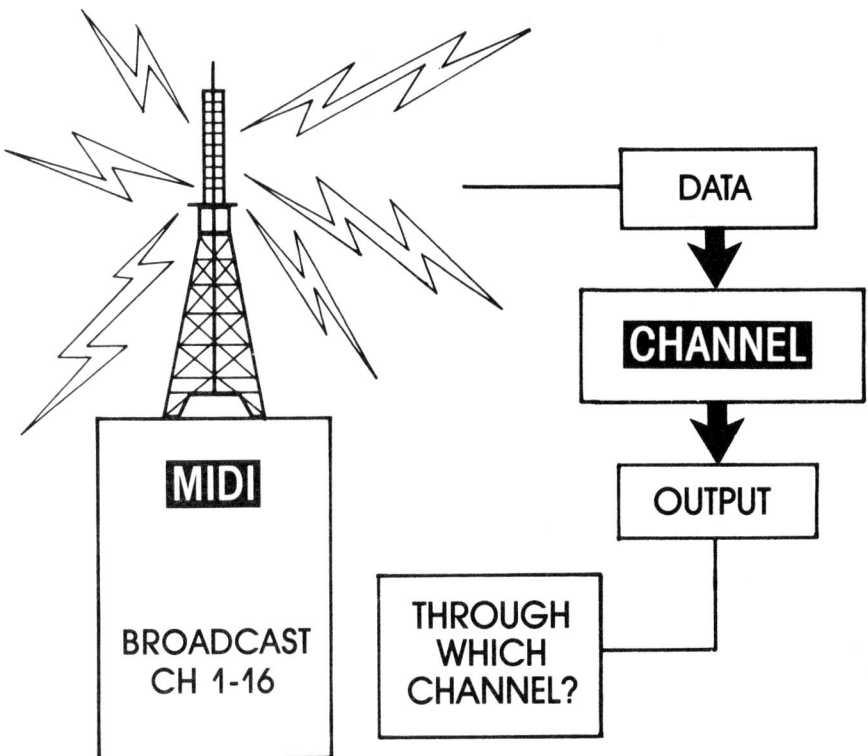

Fig. (10)

Having connected your instruments with the appropriate cable as previously described, you might expect an immediate response when you play your master keyboard. This, however, is not always the case and the reason is that MIDI communication makes use of different DATA CHANNELS.

If we consider a master instrument connected to one or more slaves, the MIDI signal being transmitted from the master might contain the following information – which key (NOTE) is being pressed (NOTE ON); being released (NOTE OFF); whether the Pitch Wheel is being moved (PITCH BENDER); and other similar MIDI messages (see fig.9). This information is transmitted by MIDI through channels numbered 1-16. MIDI can be thought of as being like a television transmitter which is sending out programmes on 16 separate channels. For the receiving instrument (or slave) to pick up the appropriate program it must be set to receive on that particular channel. With some keyboards, like the YAMAHA DX7, only one channel (MIDI Channel 1) is available for sending the MIDI commands. However, with many keyboards the transmitting channel can be selected by the user.

If we consider the example of selecting MIDI Channel 1 as the transmission or sending channel (details of how to achieve this should be found in the manual that came with your particular instrument) then all MIDI transmissions will now be sent down MIDI

Channel 1, leaving channels 2-16 silent or "closed". In order to receive these MIDI signals on your slave instrument it must have its MIDI receiving channel set to be the same as that of the transmission channel of the master, in this case Channel 1 (again consult your instrument manual for instructions on how to set the receiving channel). If you find that your slave instruments are only responding with silence, always check that the Transmit/Receive channels are set to the same number. There is, however, one exception to this. If either of your instruments supports OMNI ON then this alignment of channels is not necessary when used in this mode (OMNI ON).

OMNI in this context means "all channels". When the transmitting (master instrument) channel is set to OMNI ON the MIDI signal, like a party political broadcast, is now sent down all channels 1-16 and hence is received by any slave regardless of the receive channel setting. OMNI OFF returns the instrument to single channel transmission (in this case) so you must again make sure that the channel settings are correctly aligned.

The OMNI ON/OFF function is not available on all instruments. If your instrument does not support this function then OMNI is effectively set to OFF and you must always check that your instrument channels are correctly aligned.

Although MIDI is a universal standard and MIDI signals can be exchanged between the instruments of different manufacturers (because of the MIDI hardware and signal format), these instruments use different ways of displaying information (panel layout etc.) and unique terms are used, certain options being

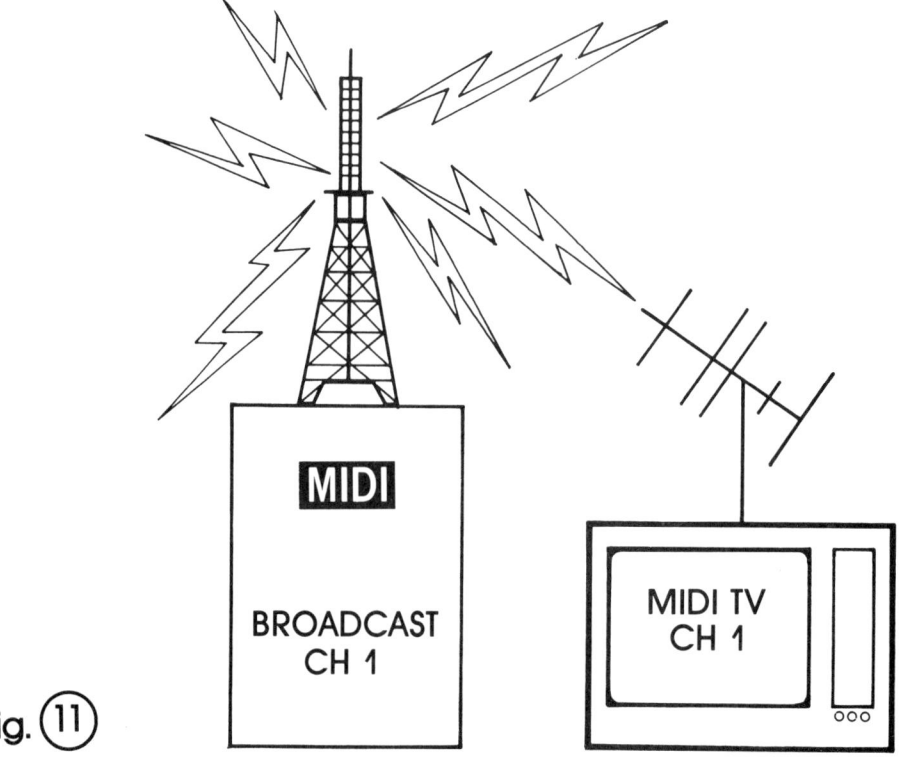

Fig. 11

MIDI BASICS

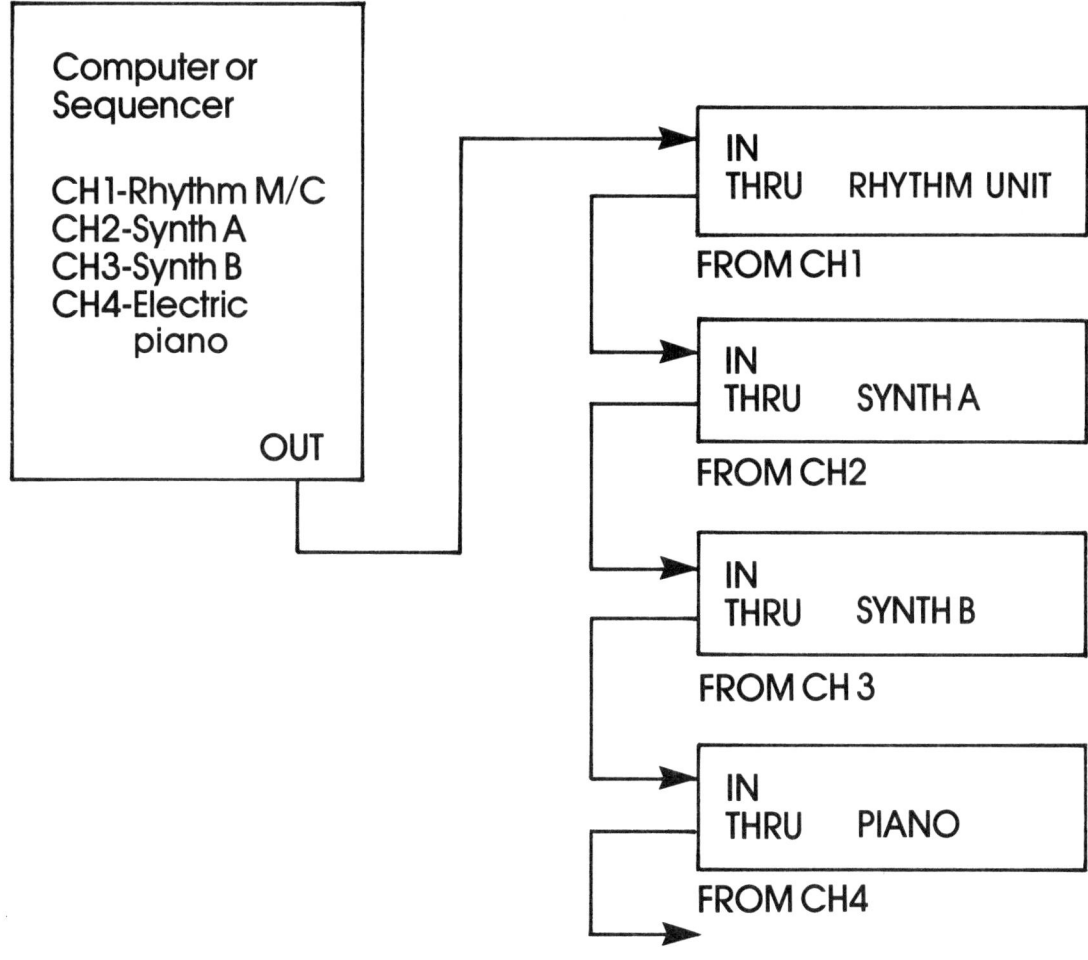

Fig. 12

supported and others not. This is a very confusing situation for beginners to master.

We will consider the case of setting the Transmit/Receive channels. On the master instrument we have various options depending on the particular instrument. The YAMAHA DX7 for example is fixed to transmit on Channel 1 only, but can be set to receive on any particular channel. With the CASIO CZ-101 both the transmit and receive channels can be set but must be the same. The YAMAHA DX 21/27 allow both functions to be set independently; other instruments also allow this but don't all support OMNI ON – fortunately in practice these problems of incompatible features can be overcome.

What then is the reason for this seemingly complicated system of MIDI channels? The advantage lies in the ability to send different MIDI signals to control many keyboards, rhythm machines (etc.) by using sequencers/computers for automatic ensemble playing. In such cases you need to send each separate instrument its own MIDI signal and by assigning separate channels you can control 16 separate instruments with a single MIDI connection. A simple example is shown in Fig.12 – a better result would be achieved using a MIDI expansion box.

13

MIDI COLUMN 2 – THE 4 MIDI MODES

The MODE messages consist of the four combinations of the MIDI commands OMNI ON/OFF, POLY ON/OFF (POLY OFF is called MONO ON). The term "message" is an alternative to the terms "command" or "MIDI data" etc. MODE MESSAGE indicates the general configuration of the MIDI messages to be sent. The MODE MESSAGE can consist of one of the following four combinations of MIDI commands.

MODE 1: OMNI ON/POLY ON
In this MODE you can play a slave (s) polyphonically without having to designate the MIDI send/receive channel.
MODE 2: OMNI ON/MONO ON
In this MODE you can play a slave (s) monophonically without having to designate the MIDI send/receive channel (if you want to send other information from the keyboard you send it using MONO).
MODE 3: OMNI OFF/POLY ON
In this MODE you can play a slave (s) polyphonically using a specific MIDI send/receive channel. This is a commonly used send/receive MODE.
MODE 4: OMNI OFF/MONO ON
If you use an 8-voice polyphonic synthesiser as a slave, effectively you can control it like 8 monophonic synthesisers. Set the voicing of each voice as desired. The channel of the master is set differently from other MODES e.g. if you set it to transmit on channel 2 you can send data for the 8 voices to be received on channels 2-9 as MONO messages. Using this MODE with sequencers very complex sounds can be created.
N.B. Synthesisers must work in a multi-timbral fashion i.e. respond to MODE 4, e.g. Casio CZ Series, Yamaha FB01, Ensoniq ESQ 1, Akai S900.

CHANNEL INFORMATION

If you look at the table in Fig.9 under the column marked Data you will find an entry marked VELOCITY (with a star after it). It is important to realise that not all keyboards respond to this MIDI data. It represents data generated by the Touch Sensitivity of the keyboard. When you press a key the value of the data that is produced depends upon the intensity of your touch. Obviously, if you wish your keyboard to respond to your touch and consequently to velocity data, it must be capable of some form of Touch Sensitivity. With the YAMAHA DX Series for example the DX1, DX5 and DX7 have this function, but it is not supported on the DX21, DX27 or DX100 i.e. the keyboard mechanism is different, the DX7 has a touch sensitive keyboard and the DX21 does not.

MIDI BASICS

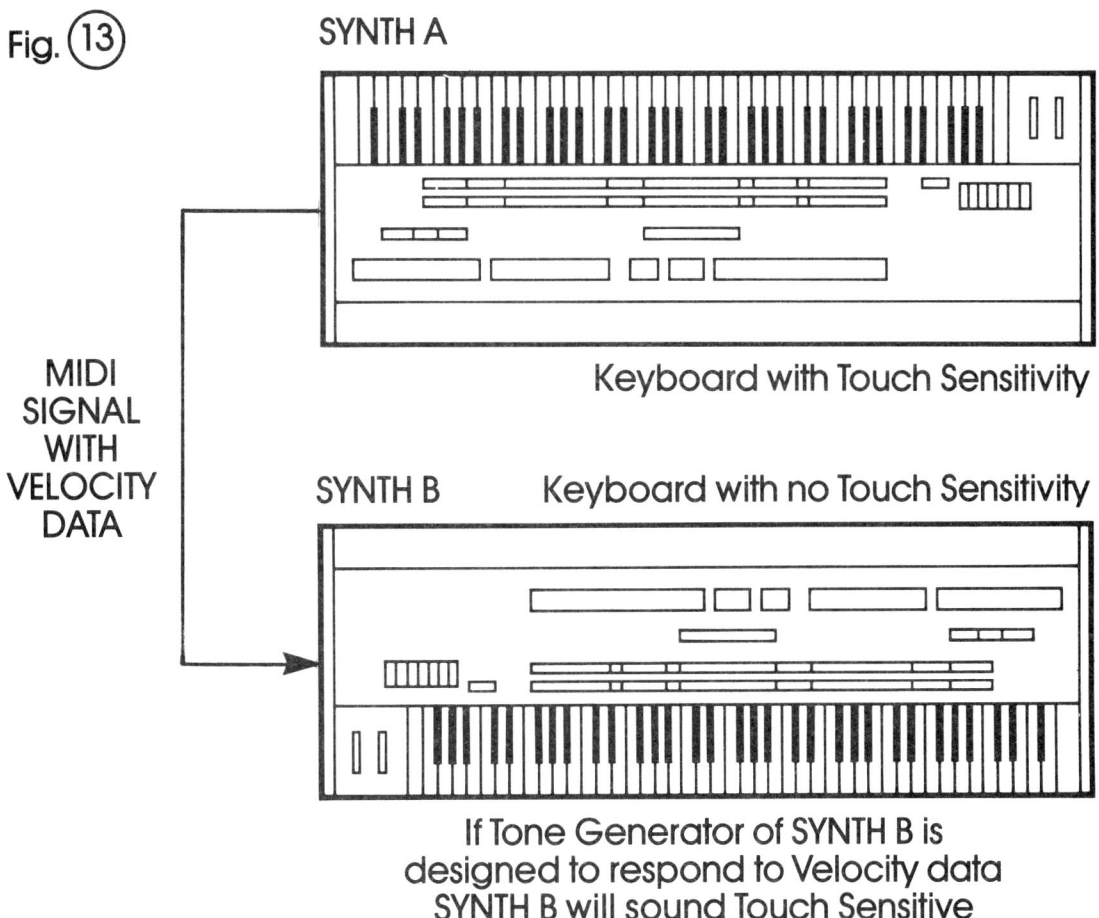

Fig. (13)

If Tone Generator of SYNTH B is designed to respond to Velocity data SYNTH B will sound Touch Sensitive

Just because your keyboard cannot generate velocity data does not always mean that it cannot respond to this data from another source. This is because the keyboard is separate from the circuitry which generates the sound. The MIDI signal communicates with this electronic circuitry and if the electronic circuitry can respond to velocity data (independent of the keyboard) you can add the effect of touch sensitivity to the sound created by the electronic circuitry.

In Fig.13 Synth A is a DX7 and Synth B is a DX27. The keyboard on the DX27 is NOT touch sensitive but if you use it as a slave of the DX7 then it is possible to play the sounds of the DX27 from the DX7 with touch sensitivity added (n.b. you have to set the voice of the DX27 to receive this velocity data).

This is not true in reverse however. If you use a keyboard WITHOUT touch sensitivity (e.g. DX27) as the master, with a keyboard with touch sensitivity (e.g. DX7) as the slave, then you will not be able to elicit touch sensitivity as the MIDI signal contains no velocity data.

Referring back to the table in Fig.9 MIDI data of the type shown is being continuously transmitted by the master to the slave instruments. Some instruments have a MIDI ON/MIDI OFF switch so if the switch is set to MIDI OFF all the MIDI functions of the

MORE MIDI DATA TYPES

DATA NAME	CONTENT
MODULATION WHEEL	WHEEL MOVEMENT
PORTAMENT SWITCH	PORTAMENTO ON/OFF
PORTAMENT TIME	TIME VALUE
VOLUME	VOLUME LEVEL
DATA ENTRY LEVEL	POSITION OF DATA ENTRY SLIDER
PROGRAM CHANGE	CHANGE OF VOICE PROGRAM NUMBER

Fig. (14)

instrument will be dead. So remember that to be able to use the instrument with MIDI the MIDI ON setting must be selected. When the switch is set to MIDI ON all the data shown in Fig. 9, which is the vital MIDI data, is capable of being transmitted to other MIDI instruments.

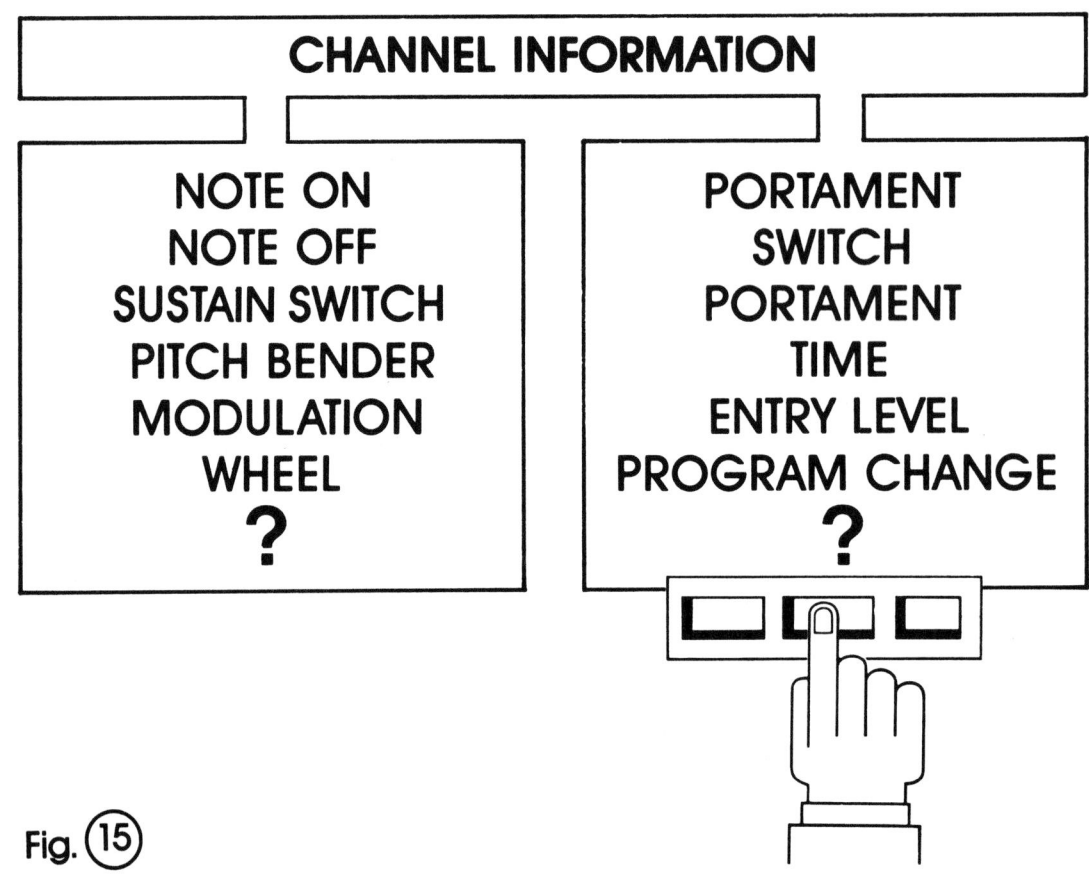

Fig. (15)

MIDI BASICS

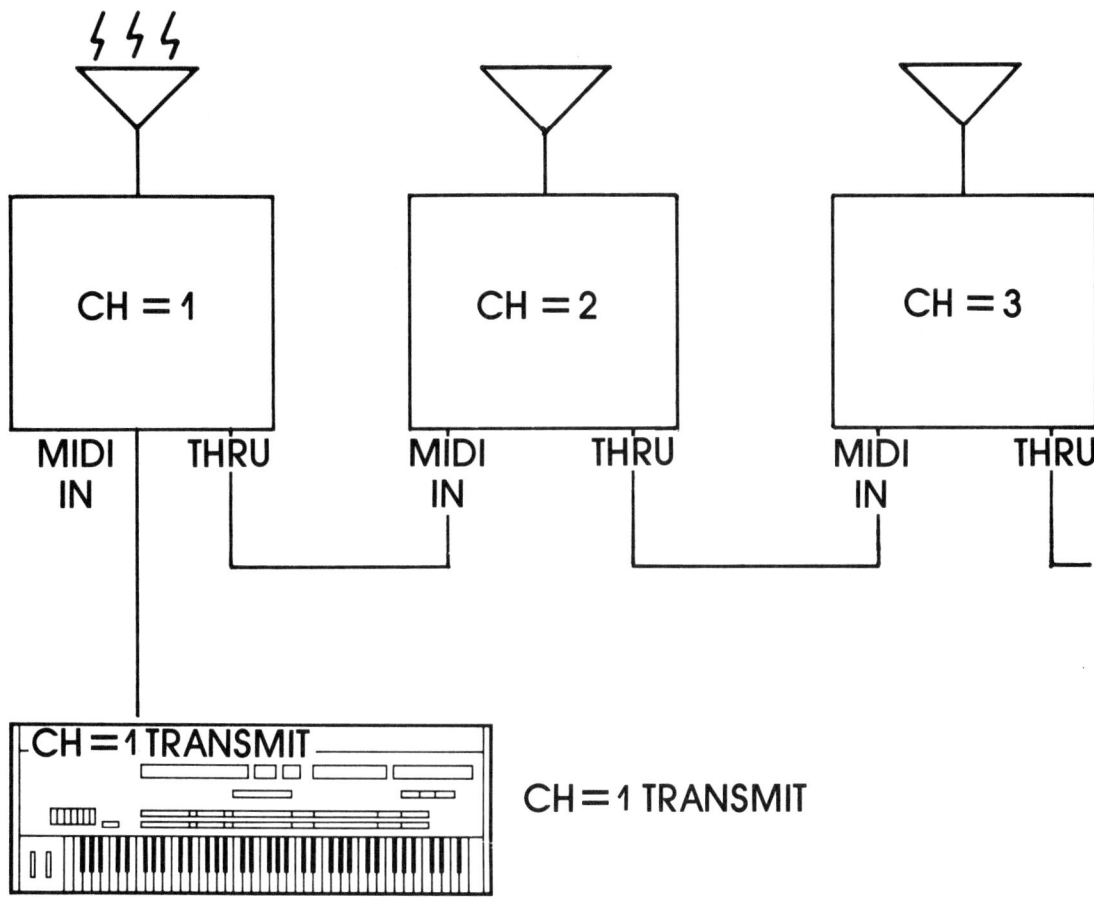

TRANSMIT ON A SINGLE CHANNEL AND INFORMATION IS NOT RECEIVED ON THE OTHERS EVEN IF THEY ARE CONNECTED

Fig. 16

The data types in Fig.9 are not the only ones available to MIDI. With MIDI ON (on both master and slave) you can select the type of MIDI data you wish to transmit. Further data types are shown in Fig.14. The decision to transmit MIDI data is made on the master and the decision to receive is made on the slave. You will begin to realise the power of MIDI when it comes to ensemble playing and the importance of sending different MIDI data according to the musical context. For example, if we consider portamento data – if you have melody playing with portamento, for a balanced and clearer sound it's unnecessary to have portamento on the backing as well. So if you have a master with portamento you can select which slaves you wish not to receive this data. The same considerations also apply to the Modulation Wheel (etc.).

The data types in Fig.14 can be switched to transmit/not transmit or receive/not receive by using the Channel Information Switch (CH.INFO). When CH.INFO is OFF on the master instrument the data is not transmitted and when CH.INFO is OFF on the slave the data is not received.

Of the data types in Fig.14, PROGRAM CHANGE is the most interesting. When you change the voice on the master instrument the voice on the slave instrument can also be changed. This occurs automatically when the voicing select button (key, switch) is pressed. This provides for quick voice changes on the master and slave instruments.

The way in which this works is that when Voice 1 on the master instrument is selected, Voice 1 on the slave is also selected. The number of the voice selected is always the same on the master and slave instruments. If, however, you want for example, to select slave voice 6 with master voice 3 then the voices on the slave instrument have to be rearranged beforehand.

If you want to create exciting combinations of instrument voices then it is well worth the effort of working out before playing how you want the voices arranged in the memory of your different instruments. If you desire to explore the MIDI PROGRAM CHANGE command it is essential that you master this aspect of your keyboards (for further details on how to achieve this see Appendix 1).

PROGRAM CHANGE commands are supported by various manufacturers' instruments, but with these different instruments the voice numbers are not the same, so you really have to experiment with PROGRAM CHANGE and find out for yourself.

All the data types shown in both Fig.9 and Fig.14 are called Channel Information, but only those in Fig.14 are affected by the setting of CH.INFO (ON/OFF). This might appear confusing but this system was decided upon when the MIDI 01. specification was first formulated. So Channel Information is a general term applied to all these MIDI messages (data types) and those shown in Fig.14 are a special section of this. Some manufacturers call the data types in Fig.9 "NOTE ONLY" and those in Fig.9 and Fig.14 "ALL DATA".

Anyway, these Channel messages (information) are very important for live work including the setting up of equipment on stage. There also exist other types of message called System messages (information) for sending and receiving voice data, which are also necessary in preparing for live performance.

Before discussing System Information we must mention more about Channel Information. With regard to velocity (Touch Sensitivity) data some MIDI keyboards do not support this MIDI function, and this also applies to portamento etc., in which case the particular data cannot be received or sent. If your instrument does not have all the functions shown in Figs 9 and 14, or indeed if it also supports additional MIDI functions, it is essential that you search through the manuals supplied to discover which particular MIDI features are implemented on your instruments.

SYSTEM INFORMATION

Although MIDI is a universal standard, not everything about it is UNIVERSAL. Different manufacturers have unique philosophies of sound creation. For example, if you want to send information about voice programming from one manufacturer's instrument to that of another manufacturer (and sometimes even of the same manufacturer) it could prove physically impossible.

In fact System Information is used for exchanging data between identical instruments or similar instruments of a single manufacturer (in the sense that they use the same voicing data). The main role of System Information (messages) is sending voice data from master to slave instruments and changing voice parameters. However, this information does not directly affect your playing; for beginners it is best to master MIDI Channel Information first and then progress to using MIDI System Information.

That concludes this beginner's seminar. Your understanding may not yet be complete but if you attempt to learn everything about MIDI at once you will end up even more confused. So just try connecting two keyboards with a single MIDI cable and experiment with the possibilities. In this way you will gradually become familiar with the use of MIDI, but remember MIDI is just another tool for the playing of music and does not guarantee musical creativity – that's up to you. Speaking personally I have a strong dislike for musicians who allow themselves to be controlled by their machines or who rely on machines to completely create their music. Machines exist for human beings, not vice versa and musicians must take up the challenge to use this greater degree of control offered, to develop their expression even more. With MIDI we can control instruments with a precision previously never even dreamed of, the important question to ask however is, how can these new facilities be integrated into your music.

MIDI IN PRACTICE

by
Akihiko Nakajima

Everybody is talking about MIDI saying that they don't understand it, but even if you don't understand MIDI fully you can still make use of it easily, this is why MIDI instruments are becoming very popular. Today MIDI keyboards are very common among keyboard players and will be even more so in the near future. MIDI entered the market place at exactly the right time, just when analog synthesisers were being replaced by digital ones. A movement to create a digital communication system for musical instruments was therefore strongly supported.

MIDI is an acronym for Musical Instrument Digital Interface and it is used for the connecting of musical instruments to each other. The MIDI standard was developed by several manufacturers from all over the world who got together to discuss musical instrument communication. So if you have a MIDI instrument then you can easily connect it to the instruments of different manufacturers if they also support MIDI. Also, this communication can be achieved with only a single cable because of the digital format of the signal.

The signal which comes from the MIDI terminals is not an audio signal, but consists of information or commands for playing. That is, you can send the information as a cypher (or code). When you play the keyboard the MIDI circuitry automatically sends this information code. For example, when you strike or release the keys or move the pitchbender or change the voice the information is sent according to the MIDI format or standard.

Playing a sequencer and rhythm machine at the same time is also controllable using MIDI, so whole systems can be created in various ways.

MIDI is available not only on keyboards and Tone Generators (expanders) but also on effects like echo and reverb., as well as drum machines, guitar synthesisers and more recently mixers and light control units. For this great variety of applications MIDI has available many different functions. All MIDI instruments do not utilise all the functions available from the MIDI standard. The concept of the MIDI standard is "when you send and receive information you need to keep to the rules laid down", but for an instrument to be considered "MIDI compatible" only a minimum number of MIDI functions needs to be supported.

MIDI has lots of advantages but also has a few drawbacks. If you want to make effective use of MIDI you have to become

MIDI BASICS

familiar with both. Starting below I am going to explain MIDI from the point of view of both software and hardware. It is much more helpful to the development of a proper understanding of MIDI if the hardware is explained as well.

Please refer to the MIDI DATA CHART on page 56 when you need the necessary MIDI numbers to send a message in practice, and to the index if you need to clarify any particular point of information.

SOFTWARE: THE MIDI TERMINAL
Connecting Instruments

If you look at different keyboards, MIDI keyboards do not have a unique or special appearance, neither do they necessarily have a superior sound. But if you look (usually on the rear panel) you will find three extra terminals – MIDI IN, MIDI OUT and MIDI THRU. These are MIDI terminals which are a unique feature of MIDI instruments, used for the transmission and reception of MIDI signals. MIDI is only of use if you have two or more instruments, so if you only have a single instrument you will not be able to make use of MIDI (yet). You might think MIDI is of value only to wealthy musicians who can afford large banks of synthesisers etc., but this is not true as you can always borrow other MIDI instruments from friends. If you do connect several MIDI instruments together then you will

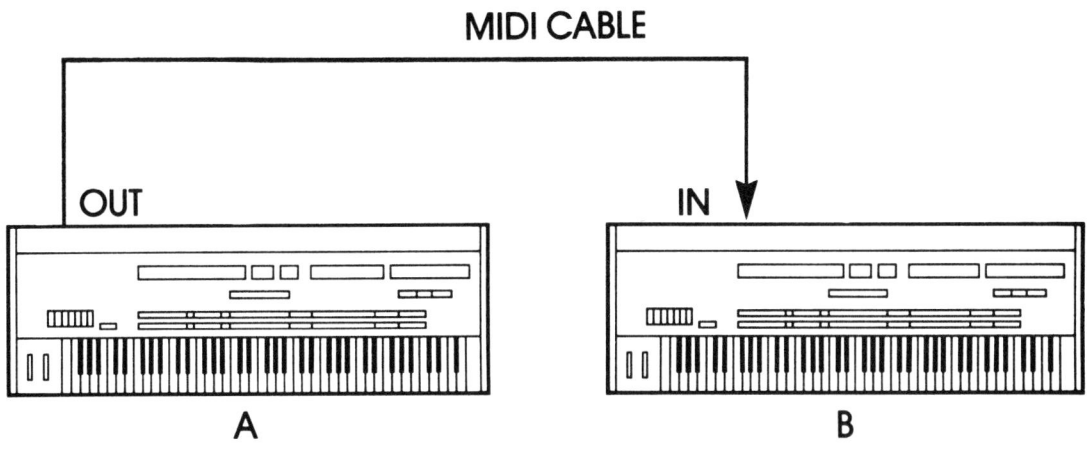

Fig. 17

really understand the value of MIDI.

The IN terminal is used for receiving the MIDI signal, and the OUT terminal is used to transmit the MIDI signal to other instruments. If you play the keyboard you can send the data generated to another instrument which will then use this data to generate its own play. For example, if you want to send a message from keyboard A to keyboard B (see Fig.17), if you connect them

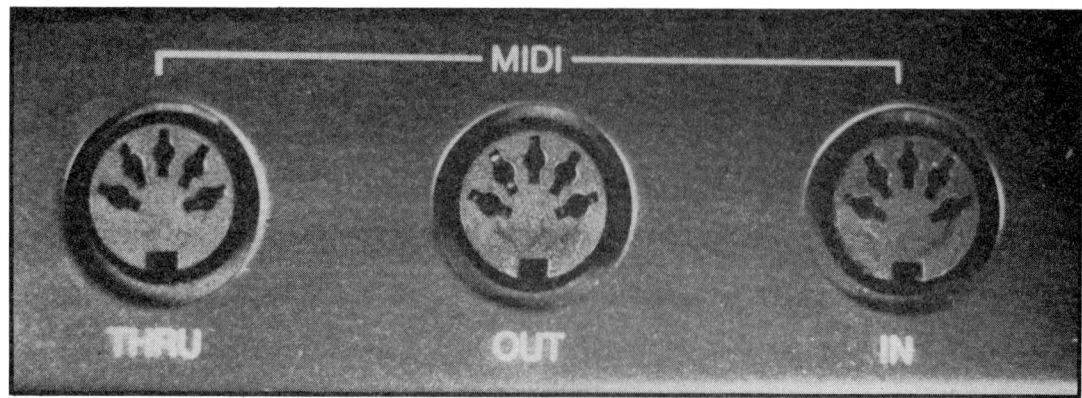

Fig. 17a

as shown with the MIDI OUT terminal of keyboard A connected with the MIDI cable to the MIDI IN terminal of keyboard B, you can then transfer information from keyboard A to keyboard B. Also, if you play keyboard A then keyboard B might simultaneously play along. Why only "might"? Because it is not certain that keyboard B will respond. In most cases keyboard B will respond, but because different machines have different configurations of voice control we cannot be sure of what will happen. The advantage of MIDI is that everybody can connect MIDI keyboards together and enjoy playing them without deeper knowledge of MIDI functions, but if you want to apply MIDI to more complex situations this is not so simple.

The THRU terminal is used to re-transmit the MIDI signal that is received by the IN terminal. If your second instrument has this MIDI THRU terminal then you can simultaneously play 3rd, 4th . . . MIDI keyboards (see Fig.18). So using this terminal you can chain instruments together, but in practice you gradually reach a point where the delay in the MIDI signal becomes noticeable. It is best to limit your instrument chains to about three instruments.

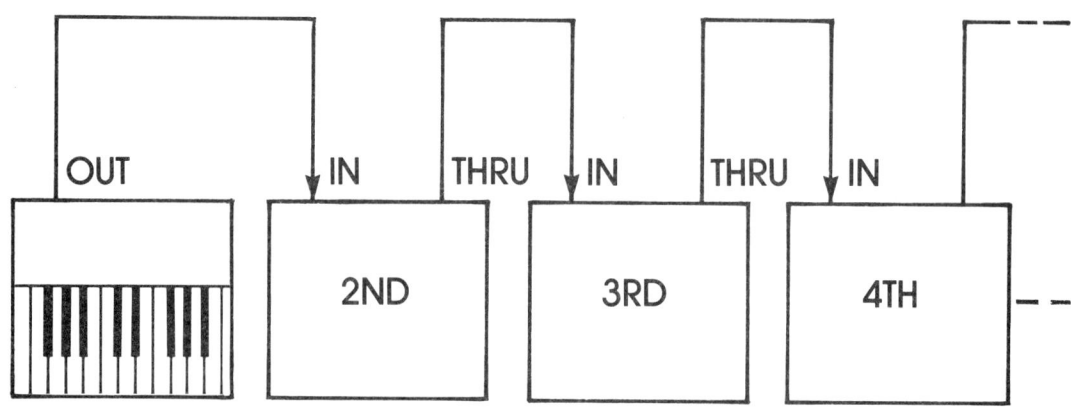

Fig. 18

MIDI BASICS

To cope with this problem effectively you need to obtain a MIDI expansion box (THRU box). This distributes a single MIDI signal via a number of parallel MIDI THRU terminals and is essential for setting up more complex MIDI systems. Fig. 19 shows a simple example of how to connect a number of keyboards using a MIDI expansion box.

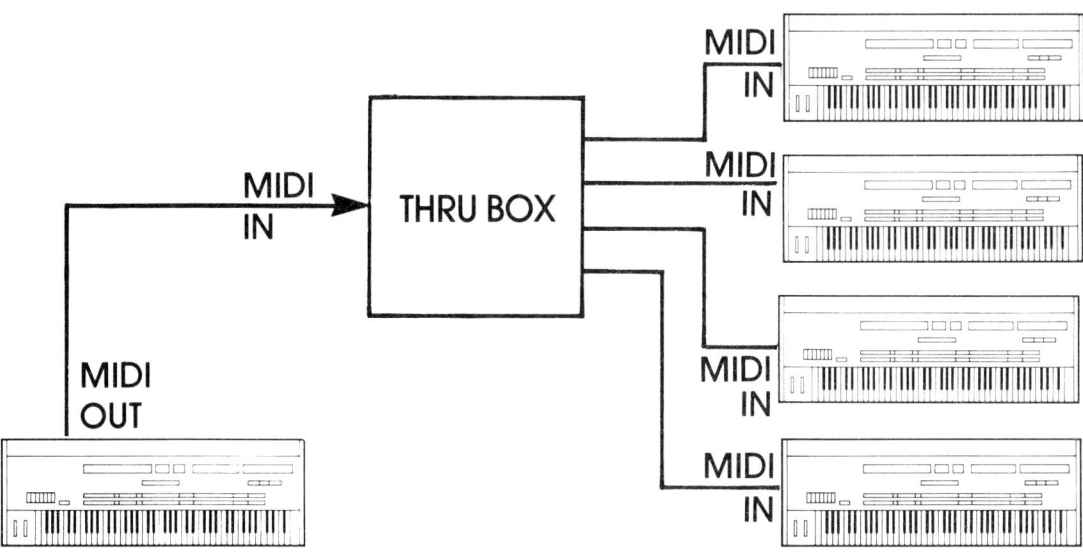

Fig. 19

HARDWARE

All MIDI keyboards contain a MIDI interface, and a microcomputer which controls the operation of MIDI. The MIDI signal is digital, which means that all MIDI instruments contain some form of digital control, so we cannot think about MIDI instruments in the same way that we think about analog synthesisers, but the final signal that MIDI instruments generate is still an analog signal. So in the process of signal transformation from the original MIDI signal to the final audio output some form of D/A conversion takes place. In other words MIDI instruments cannot be thought of as being 100% digital.

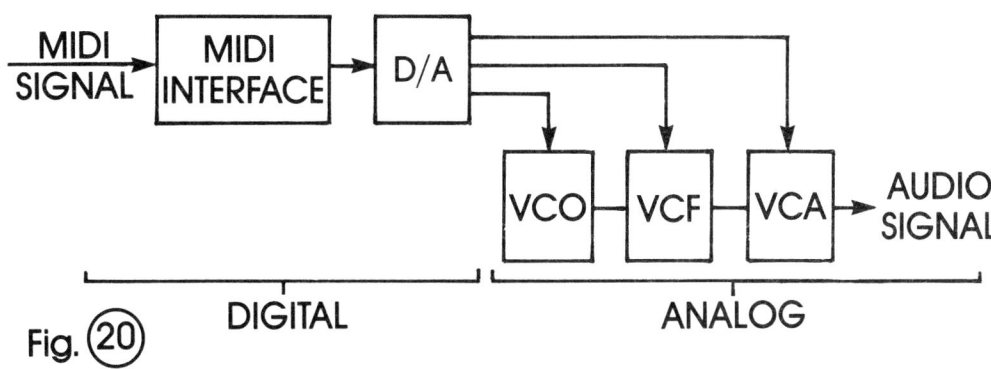

Fig. 20

With respect to the sound, after the D/A conversion the control processes are the same as for an analog synthesiser (see Fig.20). Digital control has many advantages particularly when it comes to accuracy and stability. However, some MIDI controlled instruments still have a VCO because analog control can contribute unique tone qualities (which are a result of its inherent instability).

The MIDI interface consists of a MIDI transmitter and a MIDI receiver. The transmitter sends a signal configured according to the MIDI format, and the receiver is capable of accepting such a signal. The interface uses a special IC designed especially for data communication, called a UART. The receiver circuitry is protected from electrical disturbance by an isolator circuit i.e. if the MIDI IN terminal receives the wrong form of signal energy the interface is not physically connected, so your instrument will not suffer irreparable damage.

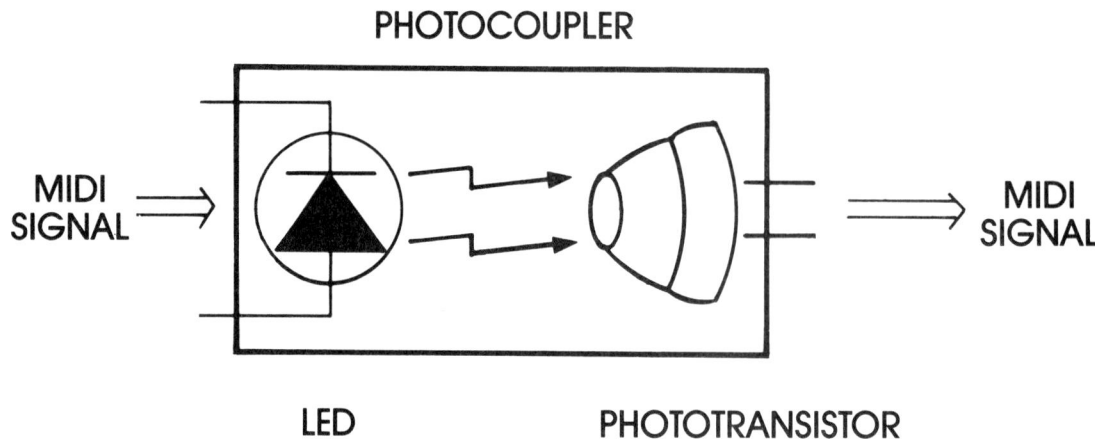

Fig. (21)   MIDI MESSAGE PROCESSED AND TRANSMITTED

This circuit utilises a photo-coupler to make the signal connection, whilst being physically separated from the internal circuitry. The photo-coupler is illustrated in Fig.21 in a simplified form. It consists of an LED and a photo-transistor. The LED converts the MIDI signal into a varying light signal which is then reconverted by the photo-transistor back into an electrical signal which is identical to the original MIDI input.

This conversion from MIDI to LIGHT to MIDI provides 100% isolation, but in the process introduces at least a 2 μsec delay. This is the reason for the difficulties encountered in chaining instruments via the MIDI THRU terminals, as the isolator circuit takes a definite time to convert/reconvert so that the pulse wave from the MIDI signal is distorted (shifted in time). In the future, by using faster photo-couplers, it will be possible to chain 10 or even 20 MIDI keyboards using the MIDI THRU terminals directly. The receiver

MIDI BASICS

circuit is a 5mA current loop type: Logical 0 is current ON (i.e. it requires less than 5mA to be turned on).

As an experiment you can connect the MIDI IN and MIDI OUT terminals on a single keyboard. Of course the effects created by voice assign will be different, but in many cases you can produce Dual voices with a thicker sound (the detune effect will not operate so the effect is very subtle).

SOFTWARE: THE MIDI CABLE
Its Structure and Length

When you connect instruments so that they can exchange MIDI signals you have to use special cable (called MIDI cable). Although the cable is especially for MIDI, it is not from a hardware point of view in any way special, in fact the cable is similar to that used for DIN connections in audio and rhythm machines, but we have to be careful because there are differences in the way the plugs are wired.

Fig.22 illustrates the 180 degree 5-pin DIN socket. The connector also has 5 pins. In fact when you exchange the MIDI signals only 2 pins (3 pins including earth) are used, pins 4 and 5 together with pin 2 which acts as an earth. Pins 1 and 3 are usually left disconnected (see Fig.23). DIN SYNC cables used for synchronising rhythm machines or sequencers (non-MIDI) usually have pins 1 and 3 connected, so if you try to use MIDI cable for such connections they often do not work, but using ordinary DIN cable for MIDI connections is usually trouble free.

Future developments of MIDI may make use of these free pins but at the moment they are left disconnected. As the MIDI signal is digital it does not suffer so much from noise problems, unlike audio

DIN PIN POSITIONS

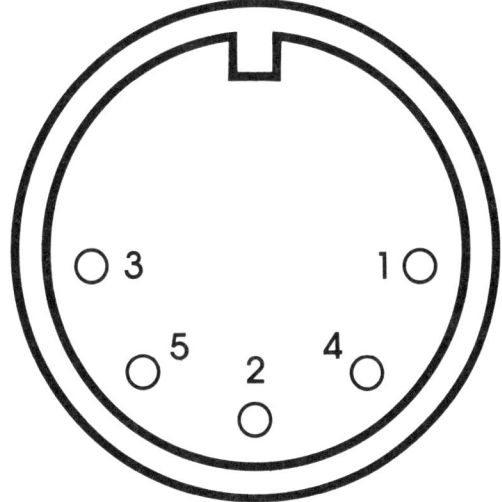

Fig.

signals which can become degraded, but if some of the MIDI signal is distorted then the effects are far more drastic than with audio. With audio there is just a loss of quality, but with MIDI if the information (signal) is changed quite unexpected results can be produced. For example, notes played can continue indefinitely or notes that you never sent will play.

	OUT	IN
1	×	×
2	EARTH	×
3	×	×
4	(+)	(−)
5	(−)	(+)

Fig. 23

The longer the MIDI cable the more likely you are to encounter problems with the MIDI signal, so the MIDI specifications recommend a maximum length for MIDI cable of 15m. In practice longer cable lengths can work satisfactorily. I have myself used 40m long MIDI cable and encountered no difficulty in exchanging MIDI signals. In fact if you use MIDI cable shorter than 15m and it is subject to a lot of movement, problems often arise. Although there are limits to the amount of DIN cable you can use, if it is well sited and kept stable you can safely use lengths greater than 15m. However, when you use a shoulder-slung keyboard on stage it's likely that problems will arise even with cable lengths of less than 15m.

Many musicians like to use longer cable or even wireless MIDI connections for greater freedom on stage. As there is a limit to how far you can extend the DIN cable, you could use a glass-fibre optical connection. You can construct one yourself and connections of up to 100m are quite feasible. Wireless connection is also possible, but as the MIDI signal needs to be more accurate than an audio signal, when used for MIDI they are very expensive and a small error can cause havoc.

MIDI BASICS

HARDWARE

As MIDI is a digital signal, variations in voltage do not affect it, but what is of significance is whether the MIDI pulse wave can be recognised or not. Noise or distortion is acceptable so long as this wave can be detected. The MIDI signal is very hardy, but sometimes the noise can be mistaken for the pulse wave. The digital signal combined with the pulse wave forms a series of data packages called characters. So if you lose even a single character the meaning of the data can be changed completely.

MIDI characters are formed from 8 bits of information. The value of each bit is determined by the existence (1) or non-existence (0) of the pulse wave (see Fig.24). In practice, for MIDI messages to be exchanged 10 bits are needed for each data package – 8 bits for the actual character plus a start and a stop bit. According to the MIDI specification the speed of MIDI message transmission is 31.25 KBaud (+/-1%) i.e. 31,250 bits per second, so if we calculate the time required to send one BYTE (8 bits) of the MIDI message we have 31.25 x 10 (8+2bits) + time taken for the MIDI circuits to act = 320 μsec.

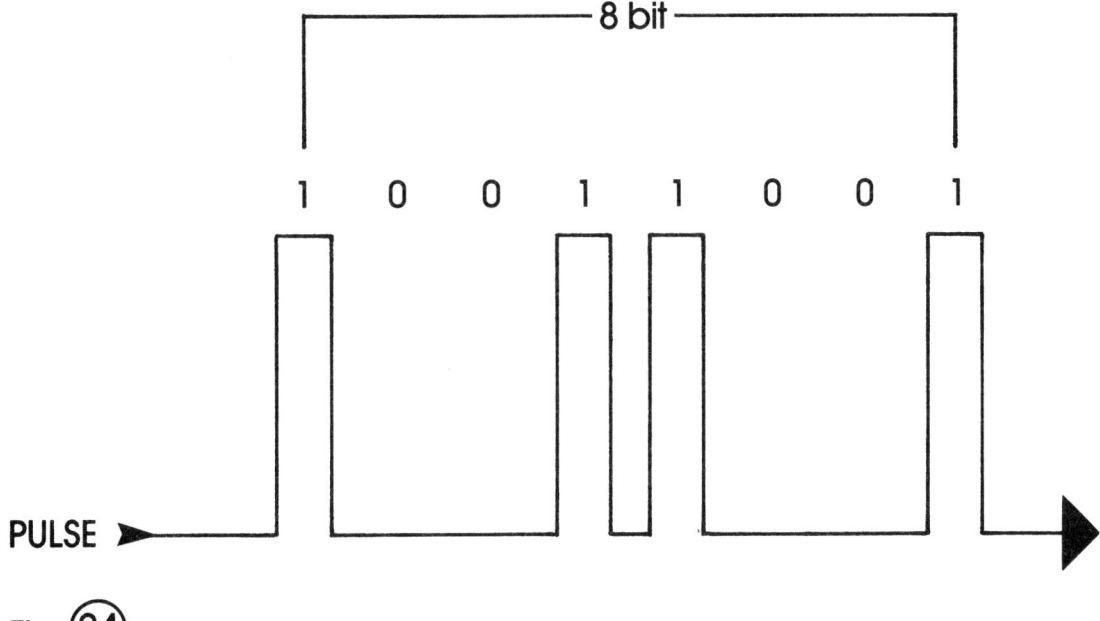

Fig. 24

320 μS is an unimaginably short time. In fact, to send the NOTE ON MIDI command, you need to use 3 bytes (Status byte, Pitch data, Velocity data) which takes 3 x 320 μS = 960 μS = 1mS. That is, if you want to make the sound of a single note using MIDI it takes about 1/1000th sec. (=1mS). In the case of serial (one after another or sequential) data exchange like MIDI, you can send a lot of different information using only a single cable – this is an advantage of MIDI. However, you pay for this because of the time

taken to deliver the message. If you play the chord of C (C-E-G) for example, the information generated (i.e. C key pressed, E key pressed, G key pressed) is sent out via the MIDI OUT terminal, the order depending upon when the keys are actually pressed and also upon how your instrument assigns key information. Even if you think that the keys are pressed together simultaneously, automatically they are placed into an order by the circuitry which scans (reads) the keyboard. Altogether it takes about 3mS to send the information created by playing the C chord.

A chord of ten notes is your physical limit, and even when you play quickly the time taken between the beginning and end of your action is greater than the 10mS taken to transmit the MIDI information, so this delay presents no serious problem. However, when you need to generate a large amount of control information, for automatic play using a sequencer or computer it is much more serious. This is especially true with rapid rhythmic play, when a time delay of about 10mS could become annoying.

Playing information is not limited to NOTE ON, there are also control messages such as Aftertouch, Pitchbend etc. all of which increase the delay. However, this source of delay cannot be avoided when we use MIDI instruments. When you use sequencers or computers with MIDI, to avoid this delay it would be very helpful to use a computer sequencer such as the YAMAHA QX1 which has 8 different MIDI OUT terminals to distribute the information, or arrange your playing so that the simultaneous data is not too concentrated.

THE RAW MIDI MESSAGE

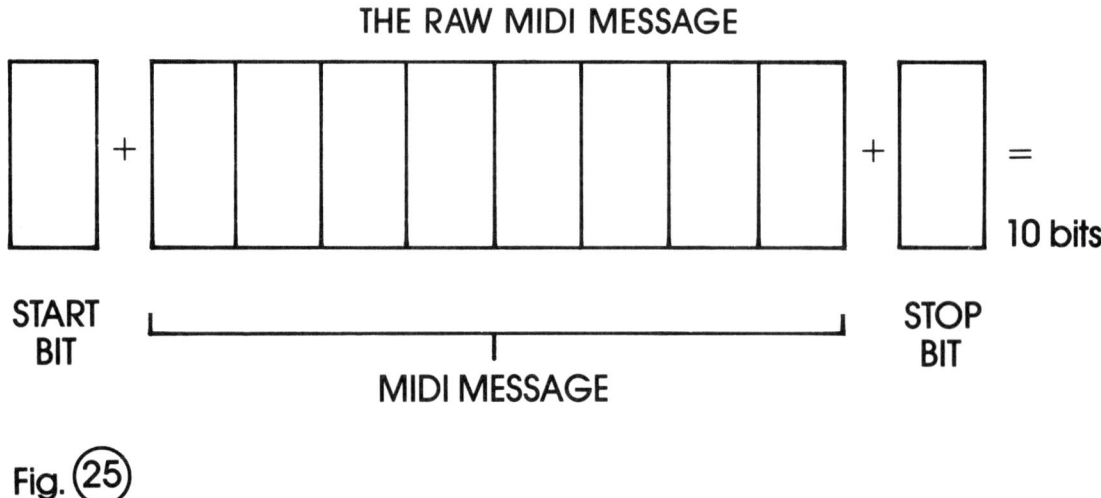

Fig. 25

SOFTWARE: MIDI MESSAGE
Requires Only A Single Cable

Before MIDI was conceived simultaneous play was possible, by using various types of CV/Gate control. When you used only one cable with CV/Gate control it was only possible to control a single function. For example, if you wanted to activate a voice on an analog synthesiser you needed at least two cables – one to carry the voltage generated by the key and one to trigger the gate to give the correct timing. In addition to this if you wanted to control dynamics or modulation etc. you had to add additional cables and if you had to control 8 or 16 voices you also needed even more cables, so if you used this system on stage the result was a riot of cables.

In the case of voltage control, large and small voltages were translated into note and modulation values etc., so if the voltage varied the notes played varied as well. It was also necessary to allow time for the synthesiser to warm up and the circuits become stable. These analog synthesisers needed about one hour before it was advisable to play them. Also there was no standard way of implementing CV/Gate control since the method of applying

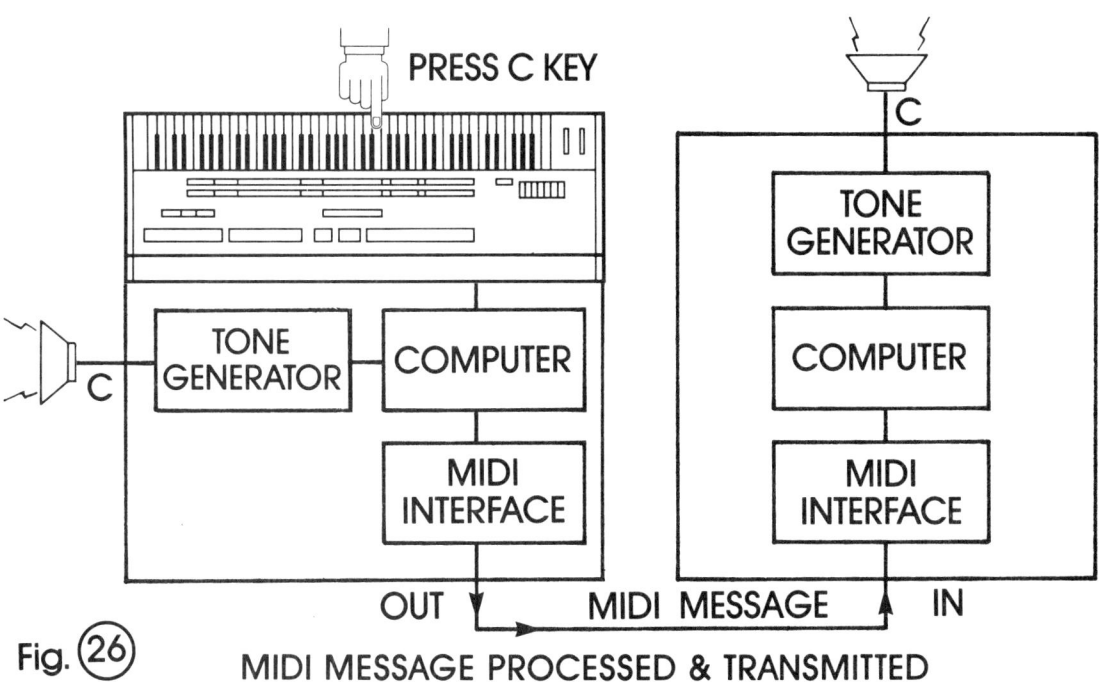

Fig. 26 MIDI MESSAGE PROCESSED & TRANSMITTED

control varied with each manufacturer, so if you wanted to connect your synthesiser to that of another manufacturer a special interface was necessary.

But MIDI is different, if you have a MIDI keyboard you can send different types of information with only one cable and also connect it to keyboards of different manufacturers. This is because MIDI uses digital signals and was designed by a group of manufacturers from all over the world. CV control uses only variations in voltage, but MIDI signals are messages containing individual characters just like a written language. Each MIDI instrument contains a micro-computer which understands these characters and controls the functioning of MIDI, that is each MIDI instrument needs its own computer circuitry to interpret and transmit MIDI signals.

This computer of course needs software, for MIDI we use a ROM which handles MIDI programming and memory storage. ROM (Read Only Memory) is a form of permanent memory which is located on an IC chip, by changing the ROM on a MIDI keyboard we can upgrade the MIDI implementation (to allow for future developments). One possible reason why this change has not yet occurred is the different functions and specifications of MIDI keyboards from each manufacturer. If you press the C key on a MIDI keyboard (see figure 26) the MIDI message takes the form of NOTE ON, followed by Pitch data, then Velocity data. If you also move the Pitch Wheel, first the channel command for Pitch Wheel is sent, followed by data which indicates the quantity of pitch bend. In such a way MIDI characters are sent, which is why you are able to send different information using only one cable.

HARDWARE

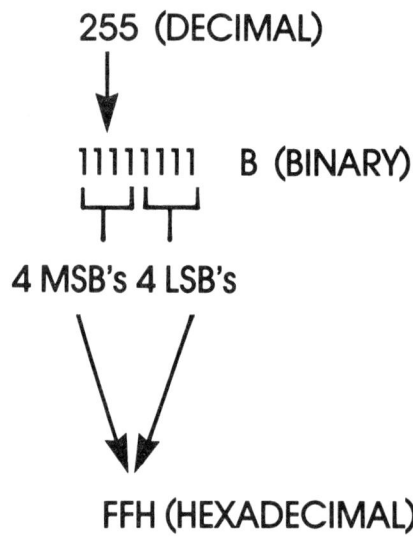

Fig. (27)

MIDI like all other digital processes utilises the special number systems – binary (numbers to the base 2) and hexadecimal (numbers to the base 16). This is because digital information has only two states, ON and OFF, and binary numbers are the most suitable for expressing the characters generated by this digital process. So the basic states generated digitally can be called 1 (ON) and 0 (OFF). The MIDI signal is carried by a pulse that is either existent or non-existent, and the smallest unit of the signal is called a Bit (Binary digit). MIDI messages come in packets of 8 bits (called a Byte) which consists of a string of 8 0's and 1's.

1 bit can be written as a single 0 or 1, for 2 bits we have 00, 01, 10, 11 which are the binary equivalents of 0, 1, 2, 3. For 8 bits

MIDI BASICS

MESSAGE CONSISTS OF 3 BYTES

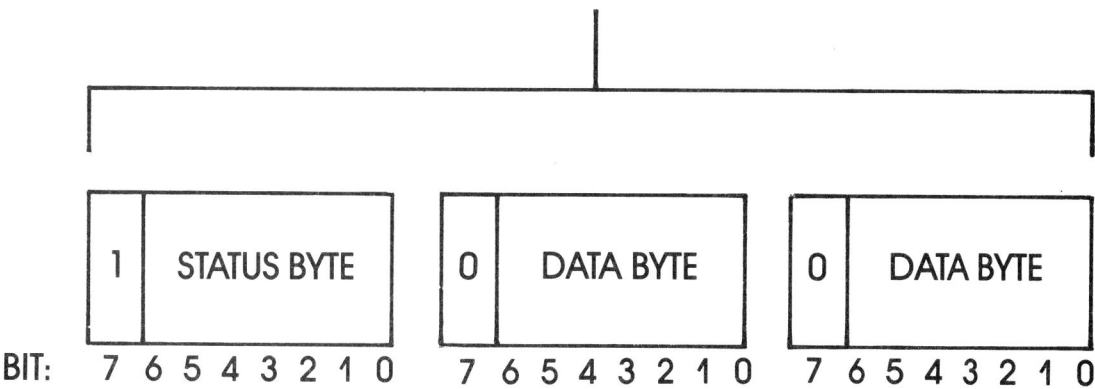

Fig. 28

we have 00000000 to 11111111 or in decimal 0 to 255. In order to indicate that a number is written in the binary form (and to distinguish it from decimal) we place a B suffix after the number e.g. 11111111B. As this binary form itself expresses the bit pattern, it makes it easy to see the form of the data, but 8 digits are a very clumsy way to express numbers, so we divide each byte into two parts. The first 4 bits are called the "4 Most Significant Bits" or MSB and the second 4 bits are called the "4 Least Significant Bits" or LSB. These half-bytes (or nibbles i.e. 4 bits) can be conveniently expressed in a number system called hexadecimal, and a suffix H is placed after a hexadecimal number so that we can distinguish it from a decimal number. If you look at the MIDI implementation chart you will find that hexadecimal numbers are frequently used in MIDI messages.

If you look at a single MIDI message you will find that it consists of a Status byte and one or more Data byte (s). The status byte tells us the type of MIDI message, and often this is followed by bytes containing the data of this particular message. The data consists of 1 or 2 data bytes, except in the case of the SYSTEM EXCLUSIVE message which usually contains more. In general the MIDI message is a status byte followed by 0, 1, 2 etc. data bytes. The 7th bit of each byte of the MIDI message is used as a flag i.e. it indicates which type the byte is – Status or Data. For a status byte the 7th bit is set to a value of 1, giving a range of values for the status byte of 80H to FFH (128–255 decimal) and for a data byte the 7th bit is set to 0 giving a more limited range of 00H to 7FH (0–127 decimal).

In the case of the data byte, if you use ordinary decimal numbers it will be much easier to interpret the data, e.g. if we change 7FH to decimal it is 127. This is the maximum value that can be carried in a single data byte by MIDI, so that NOTE NUMBER, VELOCITY, PRESSURE etc. values range from 0 to 127.

$X = 0 \sim F$

MIDI COMMAND	STATUS	1st DATA BYTE (0~7F)	2nd DATA BYTE (0~7F)
NOTE OFF	8×H	NOTE NO.	VELOCITY
NOTE ON	9×H	NOTE NO.	VELOCITY
POLYPHONIC KEY PRESSURE	A×H	NOTE NO.	PRESSURE VALUE
CONTROL CHANGE	B×H	CONTROL NO.	DATA
PROGRAM CHANGE	C×H	PROGRAM NO.	
CHANNEL PRESSURE	D×H	PRESSURE VALUE	
PITCH WHEEL CHANGE	E×H	LSB VALUE	MSB VALUE
SYSTEM EXCLUSIVE	F0H	ID NO.	ANY NO. DATA BYTES
SONG POSITION PTR	F2H	LSB VALUE	MSB VALUE
SONG SELECT	F3H	SONG SELECT NO.	
TUNE REQUEST	F6H		
END OF EXCLUSIVE	F7H		
TIMING CLOCK	F8H		
START	FAH		
CONTINUE	FBH		
STOP	FCH		
ACTIVE SENSING	FEH		
SYSTEM RESET	FFH		

Fig. 29   MIDI COMMAND Nos:

SOFTWARE: NOTE ON/NOTE OFF
The Most Basic MIDI Message

When you play a MIDI keyboard the MIDI information leaves via the MIDI OUT terminal, and the fundamental MIDI message is NOTE ON/NOTE OFF. This is a very simple message, when you press a key on the keyboard a NOTE ON MIDI command is sent followed by a NOTE OFF command when you release the key. However, you must remember that NOTE ON/OFF commands contain additional data and also that a NOTE ON and a NOTE OFF command should always be paired.

On a MIDI keyboard we often encounter the problem of a sound continuing to play after a key has been pressed. In many cases this is caused by being unable to send the correct NOTE OFF command to the slave instrument. The worst example of this occurs when the MIDI cable becomes disconnected during play, so you are physically prevented from sending the NOTE OFF commands to the slave. Many modern keyboards are equipped to handle this situation with the ACTIVE SENSING MIDI function, where the sound is automatically cut off if the MIDI cable is disconnected.

To avoid this trouble with continuous sound you should avoid changing MIDI functions while pressing the keys, as problems are

MIDI BASICS

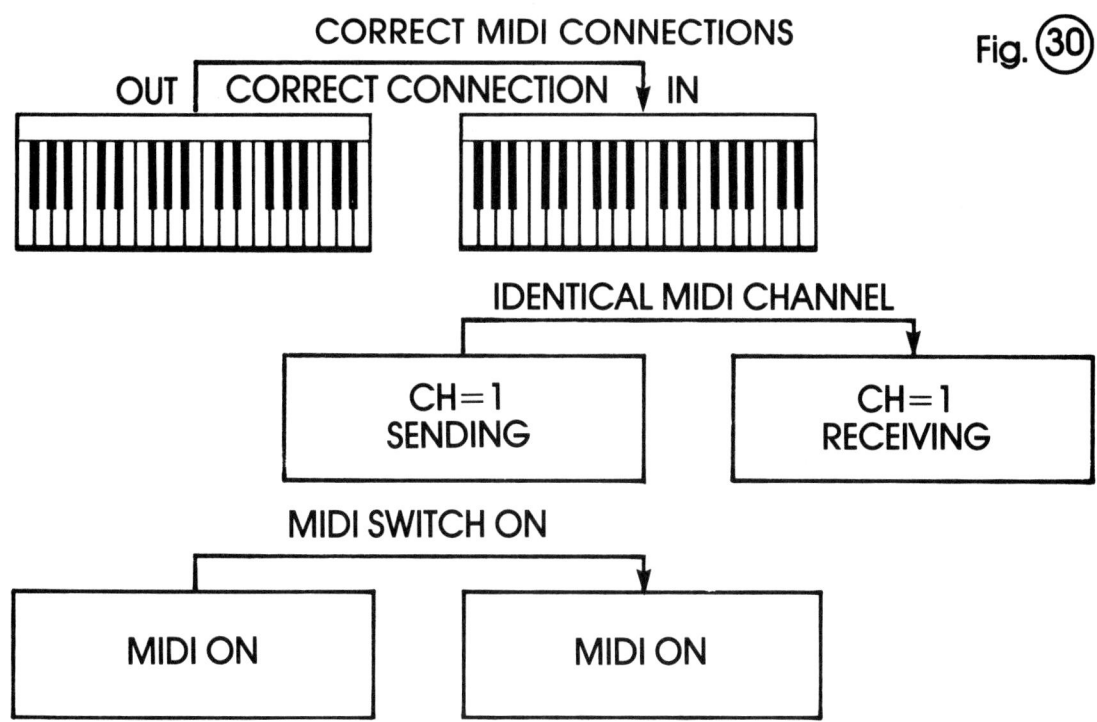

Fig. 30

often caused by exchanging MIDI channels or turning the MIDI Switch to OFF during play. These actions can also be responsible for the reverse situation where no sound is generated by the slave instrument. You should also bear in mind that unless the MIDI channels of both the master and slave are set to the same channel then information cannot be exchanged between them (we will deal with MIDI channels in greater depth later on). If you have a more sophisticated MIDI keyboard, individual parts of the MIDI signal can be switched ON and OFF, so you have to make sure that they are all turned to ON including the NOTE ON/OFF switch (this is the simplest option).

Transpose is also an important MIDI function to which attention must be paid. In general, if you press the TRANSPOSE button on the master instrument the effect is not transmitted via the MIDI OUT terminal, so you must remember to set TRANSPOSE on the slave instrument. This means that 5th degree interval play is easily achieved with a MIDI keyboard. Some keyboards however can automatically transpose MIDI messages, so transposing the slave is not necessary, but remember if you transpose before sending a NOTE OFF command you will experience a continuous sound.

The NOTE ON message also includes data specifying the pitch of the key pressed and also velocity data giving a value for the intensity of the key press. Velocity is a measure of speed, and it is the speed with which the key moves that is converted into a value for the intensity of the note i.e. if you press the key rapidly you obtain a "strong" note.

However, not all keyboards can respond to the velocity values generated by playing with different degrees of intensity. Keyboards which can respond are called dynamic or Touch Sensitive. These keyboards use different parameters to produce the velocity values (e.g. Dynamic Range), so you might have to adjust the range available to suit your playing. Some instruments contain Tone Generators which can respond to MIDI generated velocity data even though their own keyboards are not touch sensitive and don't themselves generate this data.

HARDWARE

On a MIDI standard keyboard the NOTE ON status is expressed by the number 90H and the NOTE OFF status is expressed by the number 80H (this is in the case of MIDI Channel 1). When you press a key the message NOTE ON is sent out. In more detail the status byte 90H is sent, followed by the first data byte – containing the NOTE NUMBER which corresponds to the pitch of the note – then a second data byte containing a value for the velocity.

After this, when you release the key the NOTE OFF message is sent which consists of – status byte 80H – NOTE NUMBER (same as for the NOTE ON command) – followed by velocity data. Giving a velocity value for NOTE OFF might at first seem puzzling. For NOTE ON the velocity expressed the speed of pressing the key, for NOTE OFF the velocity is used to express the speed at which the key is released. However, only a few sophisticated keyboards make use of these velocity values generated by NOTE OFF, so how this MIDI facility is applied is still largely a question of future developments.

Also included in the MIDI format is a feature called RUNNING STATUS, which allows you to omit the status byte of a MIDI message if it is of the same status as the previous MIDI message in the data stream. In this context a velocity value of 0 in a NOTE ON message is read as being NOTE OFF i.e. a 90H status byte which is followed by a velocity data byte of value 0 equals a 80H status byte. As NOTE ON/OFF messages are frequently used, if you use RUNNING

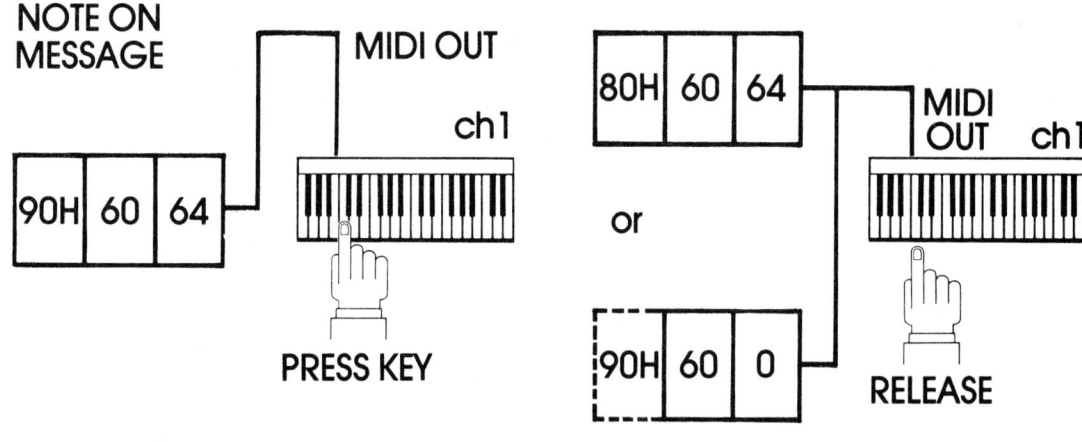

Fig. (31)

MIDI BASICS

STATUS to send your MIDI messages you can see the advantages of having only a single status byte for each "note event". In general NOTE OFF velocity values are not commonly used on keyboards, in many cases the 90H status/velocity = 0 format is used instead.

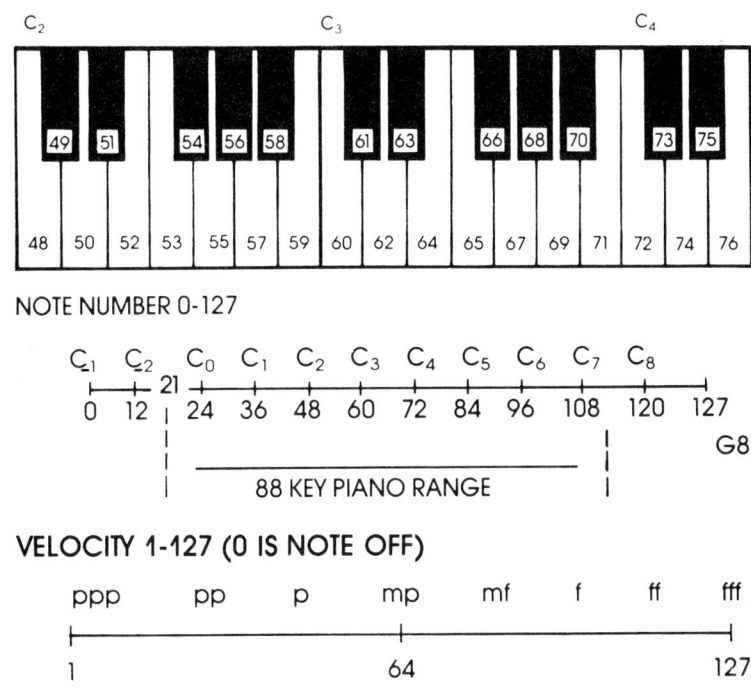

Fig. 32

Let's investigate how NOTE NUMBER and velocity values are used on MIDI keyboards. With MIDI messages each data byte can contain a value in the range 0-127. This is the case with values corresponding to the musical scale (NOTE NUMBERS). In total there are 128 note values available, C3 (middle C) forming the centre, each value being allocated a different note of the chromatic scale (semitone). The 88 keys of a normal acoustic piano in this system would have NOTE NUMBERS in the range 21-108, so we can see that more than 10 octaves are available to MIDI NOTE NUMBERS. In fact a MIDI keyboard which has a tone generator that can play the whole range 0-127 is the exception. Ranges are different on each instrument. How they react to the NOTE ON messages that are within and that are without the range of each instrument is different. In many cases they employ automatic octave shifting to solve this problem, so if the range of your slave is narrower than that of your master instrument you may experience erratic sounds from different octaves.

In the case of velocity = 0 means NOTE OFF, the range available for degrees of intensity (ppp-fff) is 1-127. Because the designs of the manufacturers and the dynamic ranges of the instruments are different ppp-fff cannot be thought of as precise levels. If a keyboard is not Touch Sensitive i.e. does not generate velocity values, then a mid-point default value of 64 is very frequently used for the velocity data bytes.

SOFTWARE: CHANNEL AND MODE
The Basic Transmit/Receive Condition

In the MIDI system the relationship between the master and slave instruments can be compared to that of a TV broadcasting station and a TV set. Like the electromagnetic wave of the TV broadcast the MIDI message is sent irrespective of the state of the receiver. In general this is called Asynchronous transmission – the sender having no knowledge of how or whether his message has been received.

Just as TV programmes are transmitted on different channels, so is MIDI. Using only a single cable we can send many separate MIDI messages which can be selected by the slave instrument by setting it to the appropriate MIDI receive channel (also called the Basic channel). This is especially useful for automatic sequencer-controlled playing where only one cable can control several instruments, because each is set to a separate MIDI channel.

If you have three MIDI keyboards for example, with each channel set as shown in the diagram (fig. 33) and set them to play different voices; e.g.
CH1: Melody
CH2: Chordal Accompaniment
CH3: Bass Line

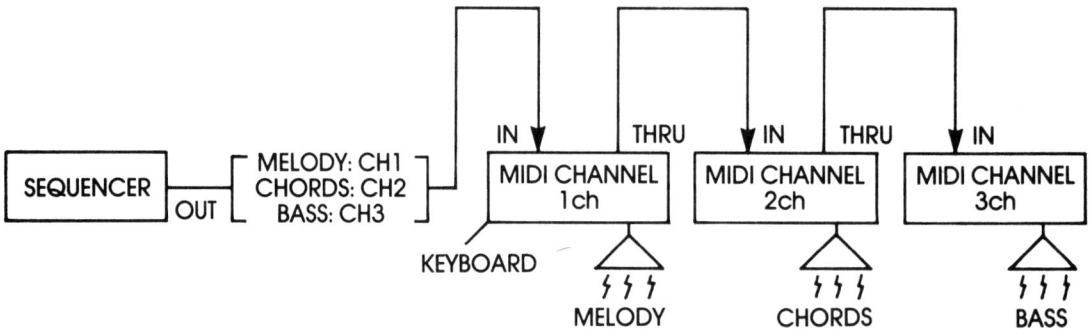

Fig. 33

each keyboard will then only play the sequencer data sent on its own particular MIDI channel.

When you connect up MIDI instruments the result is occasionally silence. One of the main reasons for this is that the MIDI transmit/receive channels are not correctly aligned. As well as being able to set individual MIDI receive channels the OMNI mode is also available which enables you to produce sounds even if you don't understand the working of MIDI channels. If you select OMNI mode ON after switching the power ON, you will never experience the silence caused by incorrect channel alignment. So this mode is very suitable for people with little experience of MIDI.

MIDI BASICS

For a while the way that manufacturers implemented the MIDI standard was to switch to a default setting of OMNI ON at POWER UP. Now, however, the trend is toward restoring the MIDI settings memorised when the instrument was last switched off, because of the convenience of reactivating your system the instant you switch on.

The relationship between MODE and Channel in MIDI is one of the most difficult concepts we have to understand. The parameters which define the MIDI MODE are:

OMNI mode ON/OFF
POLY mode ON/MONO mode (POLY mode ON/OFF)

giving us the 4 possible MODES which result from the combination of these 2 sub-modes (OMNI and POLY). The OMNI sub-mode decides if MIDI channel(s) have been selected, that is MIDI messages only use channel(s) if OMNI is set to OFF. The POLY sub-mode literally indicates that the keyboard is acting polyphonically. Its inverse MONO mode switches the instrument into a monophonic keyboard. In general if you send a message in MODE1:OMNI ON/POLY you can produce sound.

If you want to send a message using a MIDI channel you should select MODE3:OMNI OFF/POLY. To find out in more detail about the 4 MIDI MODE's for both sending and receiving please refer to the chart (fig. 37).

HARDWARE

It is not necessary for all MIDI messages to contain channel information. You can include channel information only if the status byte is in the range 8nH – EnH (from NOTE OFF to PITCH BEND). These MIDI messages are called Channel messages (as opposed to System messages). The Channel information is included in the 4LSB's (Least Significant Bits – 0-3) of the 8 bits of the status byte (see Fig.34). As you can see from this chart 4 bits give 16 possible numbers (0-15), enabling us to specify uniquely the 16 channels required by the MIDI specification – 1-16 (n.b. MIDI Channel 1 has a status byte channel value of 0 etc.).

Channel messages are divided into two types – Voice messages and MODE messages. In theory MODE messages are just one part of CONTROL CHANGE messages because their role is to define the basic character of the instruments. With a Channel message the channel information is utilised or not depending on the MODE the slave instrument receiving this message is set to. However, with MODE messages channel information is always received regardless of the MODE of the slave instrument.

	bit	1ch	2ch	3ch	4ch	5ch	6ch	7ch	8ch	9ch	10ch	11ch	12ch	13ch	14ch	15ch	16ch
4LSB's	0	0	1	0	1	0	1	0	1	0	1	0	1	0	1	0	1
	1	0	0	1	1	0	0	1	1	0	0	1	1	0	0	1	1
	2	0	0	0	0	1	1	1	1	0	0	0	0	1	1	1	1
	3	0	0	0	0	0	0	0	0	1	1	1	1	1	1	1	1
STATUS	4																
	5																
	6																
	7																

CHANNEL INFORMATION

Fig. (34)

In MIDI, MODE change is achieved using a CONTROL CHANGE message, status byte BnH with data byte values 124-127. In Fig.35 when you send a chord C-E-G on the master instrument to a slave set to Basic Channel 2 you can see the result in each of the 4 MODES. How the MODE affects both MIDI transmission and reception is fully described in the MODE chart (Fig.37). MODE4.

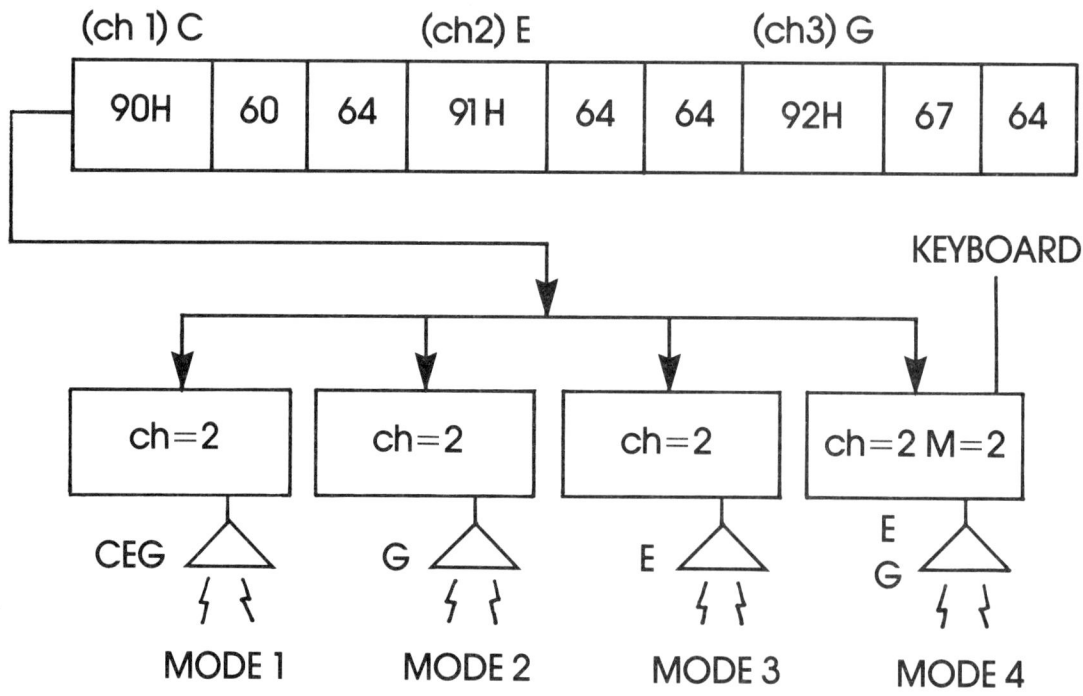

THE 4 MODES IN PRACTICE

Fig. (35)

OMNI OFF/MONO is the least used MODE. The parameter (M) is expressed as the value of the 3rd byte of the MONO MODE ON message. Each channel receives each voice from Basic Channel to Basic Channel+M–1. In other words this means you have the equivalent to M monophonic synthesizers.

MIDI BASICS

When you send a message in MODE 4 each note of a voice is assigned a separate channel, so if you want to play a chord with each note having a separate slave instrument you set the master keyboard to MODE 4 (see Fig.36 Monophonic sampler).

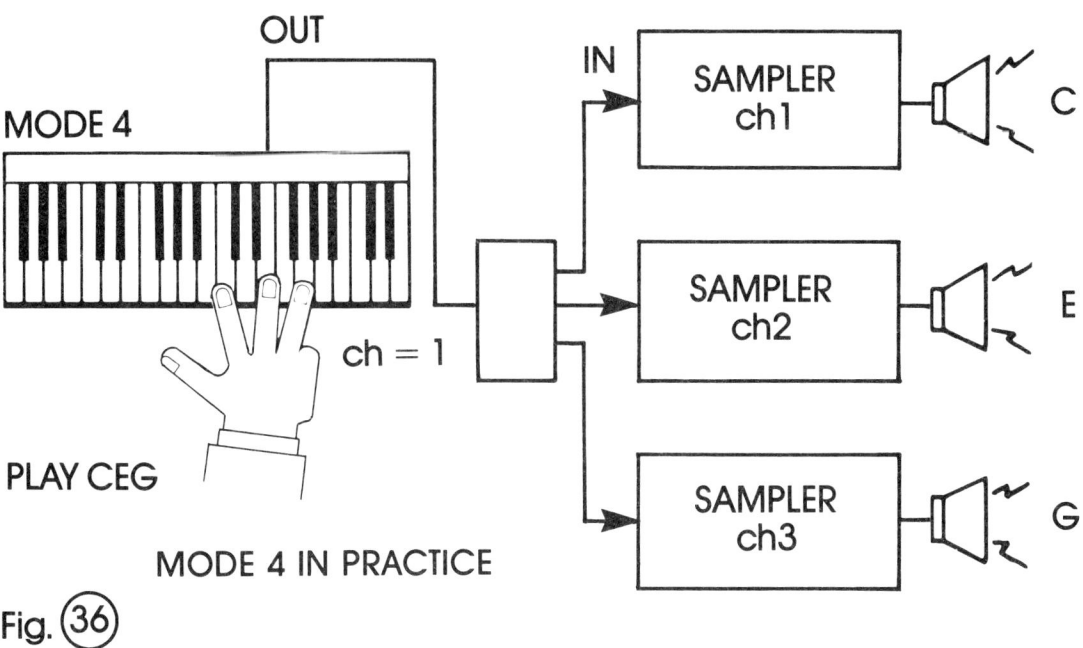

MODE 4 IN PRACTICE

Fig. 36

			MIDI OUT	MIDI IN
O M N I	POLY ON	MODE 1	ALL VOICE MESSAGES ARE SENT IN A SINGLE BASIC CHANNEL	VOICE MESSAGES FROM ALL VOICE CHANNELS ARE RECEIVED AND MATCHED WITH THE ASSIGNED VOICES POLYPHONICALLY
O N	MONO ON	MODE 2	VOICE MESSAGES FOR ONE VOICE ARE SENT IN A SINGLE BASIC CHANNEL	VOICE MESSAGES ARE RECEIVED FROM ALL VOICE CHANNELS AND CONTROL ONLY ONE VOICE
O M N I	POLY ON	MODE 3	VOICE MESSAGES FOR ALL VOICES ARE SENT IN A SINGLE BASIC CHANNEL	VOICE MESSAGES FROM VOICE CHANNEL N ONLY ARE RECEIVED AND MATCHED WITH THE ASSIGNED VOICES POLYPHONICALLY
O F F	MONO ON	MODE 4	VOICE MESSAGES FOR VOICES 1 thru M ARE SENT IN VOICE CHANNELS N thru N+M−1 RESPECTIVELY (Single Voice per Channel)	VOICE MESSAGES ARE RECEIVED IN VOICE CHANNELS N thru N+M−1 AND ASSIGNED MONOPHONICALLY TO VOICES 1 thru M RESPECTIVELY

MODE CHART

Fig. 37

SOFTWARE: AFTERTOUCH
How To Use It Depends On Your Instrument

When you play a keyboard pushing the keys horizontally, some keyboards respond with vibrato – this is called Aftertouch. How you make use of Aftertouch depends on the facilities available on your particular instrument. In many cases we can make use of Aftertouch to provide vibrato, growl, EG. bias, or tremolo etc. Of course if your keyboard does not support such a function the

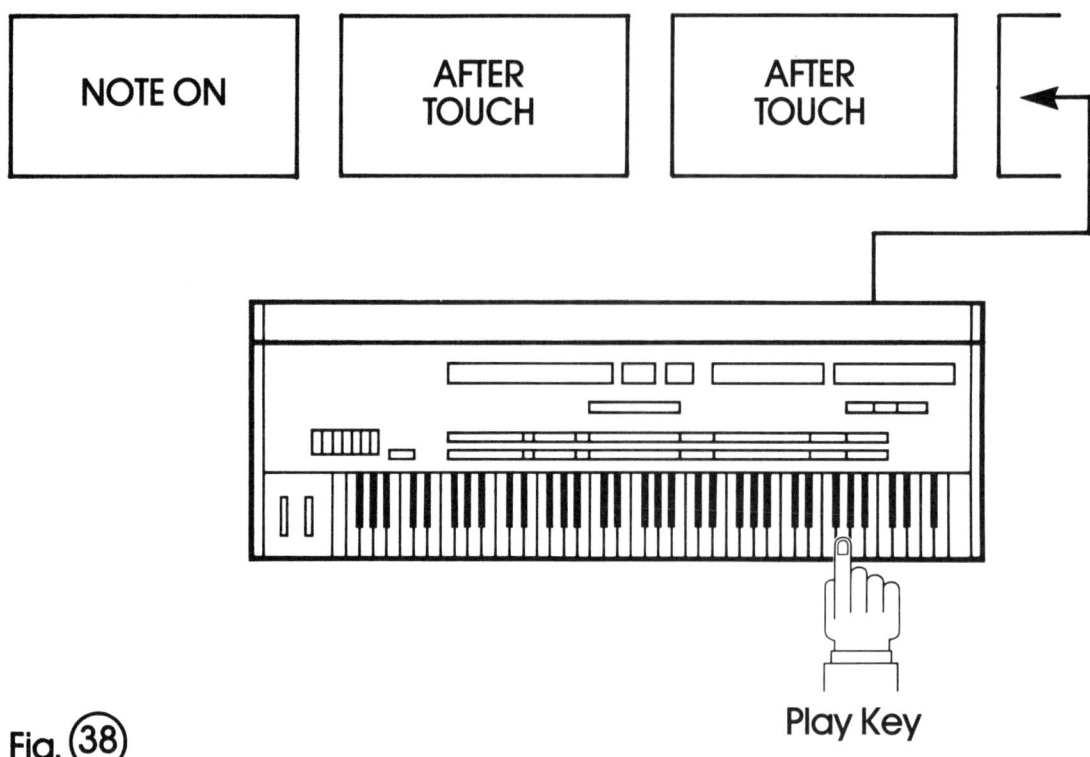

Fig. (38)

corresponding MIDI data is not sent or responded to.

If you set the Aftertouch to generate a vibrato effect on your keyboard and then play a chord (e.g. C-E-G) and push the G key "deeply", you will hear the effect not only on G but also on the C and E notes as well (automatically). This happens because on many keyboards vibrato is not available for each voice independently. However, some of the more sophisticated keyboards do provide independent vibrato for each key.

HARDWARE

In the MIDI standard there are two forms of Aftertouch using status bytes AnH and DnH. DnH is termed Channel Pressure and affects the whole instrument (keyboard) rather than particular notes. In general the term Aftertouch refers to Channel Pressure. This information is sent as a pressure value in the range 0-127; in a single data byte following the status byte DnH.

AnH is called Polyphonic Key Pressure, which can provide Aftertouch effects on each key independently. This uses 2 data bytes after the status byte AnH, a NOTE NUMBER and a Key Pressure value.

Aftertouch information is sent much more frequently in the MIDI data stream compared to NOTE ON/NOTE OFF commands, because every slight change of pressure will send MIDI data. This data is often sent unknowingly by the keyboard player. Just by changing the way the key is pressed, this information is automatically sent by any MIDI keyboard with Aftertouch. Of course, compared with Channel Pressure, Polyphonic Key pressure is much more expressive musically. As it sends information about each key independently you may send more than 20 times as much information to achieve the desired result. In general, Aftertouch is quite often used but Polyphonic Key Pressure is only supported by the most advanced and sophisticated keyboards.

In the case of real time recording e.g. MIDI sequence recorders, you will need a lot of memory to make use of MIDI Aftertouch data, so some keyboards allow you to control this Information. When you come to overdub your music avoid using too much Channel Pressure, or the data will become confused and your play messy.

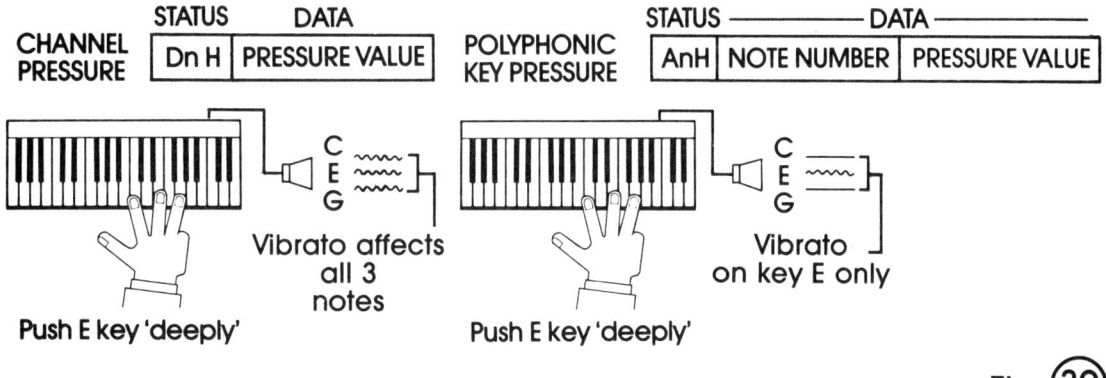

Fig. 39

SOFTWARE: PROGRAM CHANGE
How To Achieve PROGRAM CHANGE On Various Synthesisers

When you push a Voice Select button on a keyboard, PROGRAM CHANGE information is sent, enabling you to change the voices on more than one keyboard automatically. PROGRAM CHANGE does not only apply to keyboards, but different Delay/Reverb settings on digital MIDI effects units also use this function. If you set up Program Numbers beforehand then the amount of delay for example can be automatically changed simply by changing voices on your master instrument.

The way voices are numbered varies for different instruments (e.g. 00-99, 1-24 in Banks A-D etc.). Of course it's very easy if you have only one type of keyboard, but if you use several different types of keyboard then you have to learn the various ways of arranging Voice Numbers beforehand. Also with MIDI it is possible to select between 128 Programs with the MIDI Program Change command. If your instrument's voice memory contains more voices than this, then you cannot access more than 128 of them at any one time.

Some synthesisers have a Voice Select button which incorporates a Voice Memory Dump function (enabling the

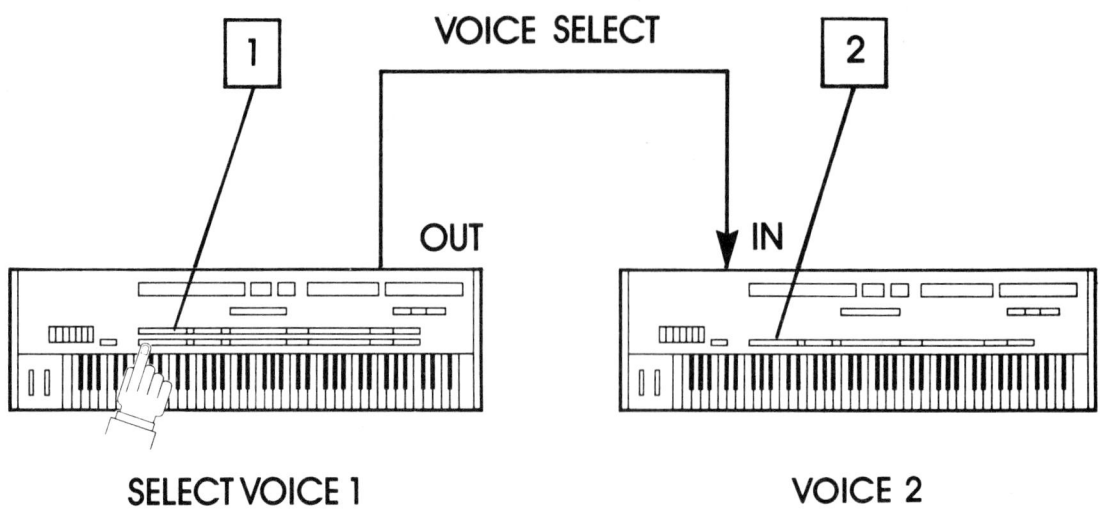

Fig. 40

transfer of voice data between two keyboards of the same type), but you cannot execute both PROGRAM CHANGE and Memory Dump simultaneously, so that when the Dump function is operating PROGRAM CHANGES cannot be sent.

HARDWARE

When you push a Voice Select button a MIDI PROGRAM CHANGE command is sent. If the Basic Channel is CH1, following the status byte C0H, a PROGRAM NUMBER in the range 0-127 is sent in the next data byte, so that the Voice Number displayed

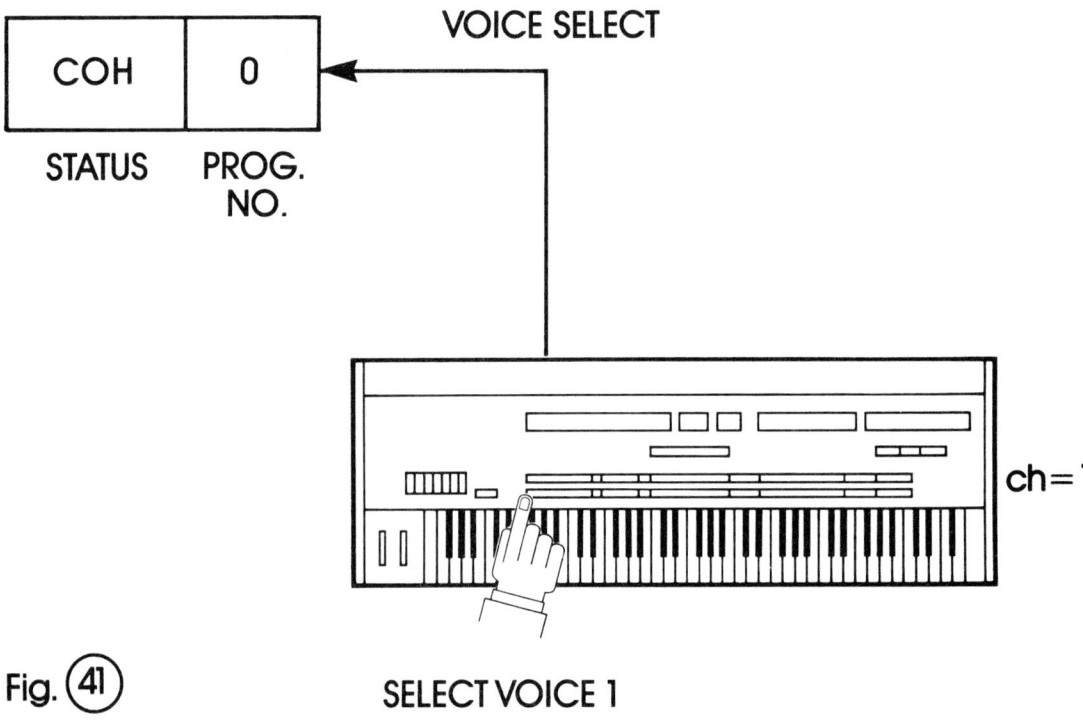

Fig. 41   SELECT VOICE 1

on the keyboard panel is very probably not the same as the MIDI PROGRAM NUMBER. Even if the Voice Number is 1-32, or A-F etc., it is always allocated to a range of 0-127 for MIDI transmission. How to assign the Voice Numbers is decided freely by different manufacturers. In order to connect different manufacturers' instruments or machines you must become familiar with the Voice Number configurations beforehand.

MIDI COLUMN 3
Rhythm Machine/Sequencer Synchronisation.

All MIDI standard drum machines contain a built-in sequencer for automatic rhythm play. The individual instruments of each drum machine are allocated a MIDI NOTE NUMBER, so that you can control these instruments from an external source with NOTE ON messages. Of course it is also possible to play a suitable drum machine from the keys of a MIDI keyboard, but in general in an

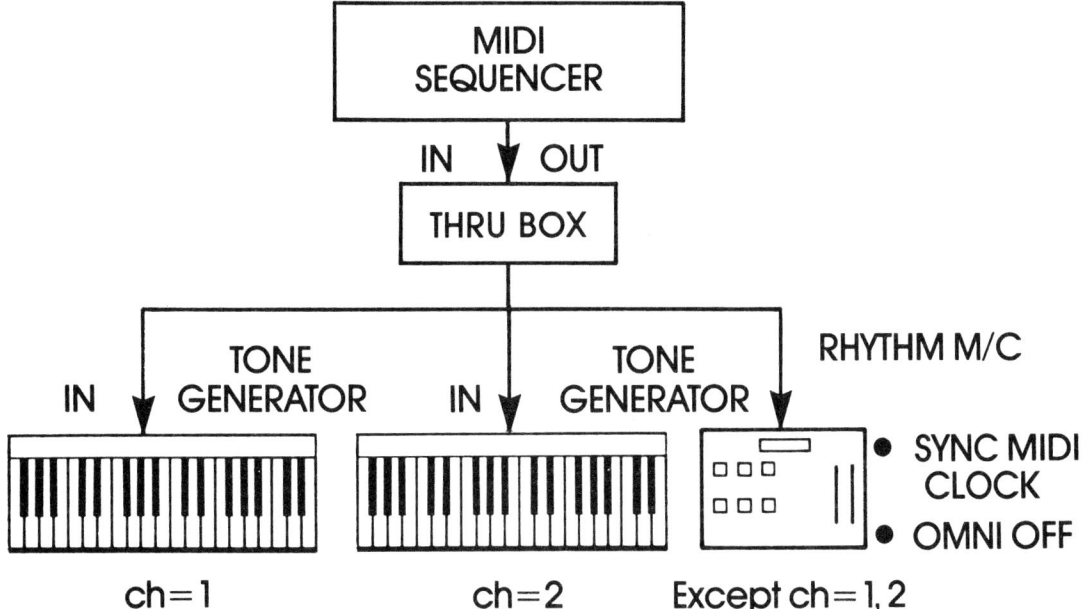

Fig. 42   RHYTHM MACHINE/SEQUENCER SYNC

automatic play system we very often synchronise the built-in sequencer of the drum machine to the MIDI CLOCK of the external control source – we don't very often directly control the individual instruments of a drum machine. To synchronise the built-in sequencer of a drum machine to MIDI CLOCK, set SYNC. to MIDI CLOCK. Because the NOTE ON message is used to play synthesisers etc., to avoid the drum machine receiving these messages and making sound you need to set OMNI OFF or to set a MIDI Basic Channel which you are not using.

SOFTWARE: CONTROL CHANGE
The Organisation Of Controllers

The degree of effect generated by controllers such as Modulation wheels, Volume pedals, Damper and Breath controllers is expressed by the CONTROL CHANGE MIDI message. Each effects controller is assigned a number (CONTROL NUMBER) which is used for that particular controller. However, as each instrument has different types of controllers, the meanings of specific CONTROL NUMBERs are not necessarily identical. In general when you move the Modulation wheel it is likely that you can create a modulation effect on your slave instrument. This is not because of any particular agreement, but because manufacturers have tended to fall into line behind the major producers.

If your keyboard allows you some form of MIDI Controller assign function then you will be able to allocate the CONTROL NUMBERs as you wish. This type of keyboard has the flexibility to cope with most varieties of MIDI instrument, as well as allowing a more variable and flexible combination of different controllers e.g. controlling the Damper with the Modulation Wheel of the master. It depends on your needs as to how you set up the CONTROL NUMBERs. The chart below (Fig.43) shows the function of the common or principal CONTROL NUMBERS.

CONTROL NUMBER	
1	MODULATION WHEEL
2	BREATH CONTROLLER
3	AFTER TOUCH
4	FOOT CONTROLLERS
5	PORTAMENTO TIME
6	DATA ENTRY
7	VOLUME
64	SUSTAIN PEDAL
65	PORTAMENTO PEDAL
66	SOSTENUTO
67	SOFT PEDAL
96	DATA + 1 (INCREMENT)
97	DATA − 1 (DECREMENT)

MIDI CONTROL Nos:

Fig. 43

HARDWARE

The CONTROL CHANGE MIDI command consists of the status byte BnH, followed by a data byte containing the CONTROL NUMBER indicating the type of effect, then a second data byte indicating the degree of effect. CONTROL NUMBERs 0-31 are allocated to what are termed continuous controllers which change analog to digital values generated by sliders or wheels etc. In situations where a greater degree of accuracy is required, controllers assigned to CONTROL NUMBERs 0-31 can use numbers 32-63 as the Least Significant Bit. CONTROL NUMBERs 64-95 are assigned to switch controllers (ON/OFF). In general switch ON uses a value of 127 and switch OFF a value of 0.

More recently however, the distinction between continuous and switch controllers is becoming less obvious and in the future cheaper switch types may be substituted for continuous controllers. As a consequence, more central values are being used. CONTROL NUMBERs 96-121 are left undefined and can be allocated to special uses.

With the CONTROL CHANGE MIDI message we can control controllers which have been allocated the same CONTROL NUMBER. Even if the master and slave instruments have the same controller functions we cannot exercise control unless they have the same CONTROL NUMBER.

BnH	CONTROL NUMBER	DATA

Fig.  CONTROL CHANGE MIDI COMMAND

CONTROL NUMBERs 122-127 are called Mode messages with 124-127 handling MODE change (OMNI mode ON/OFF and POLY mode ON/MONO) see Fig.45. 122 is LOCAL CONTROL, if you set it to OFF then the keyboard of the instrument does not generate a sound, but the Tone Generator can still be controlled by MIDI, also if you then play the keyboard MIDI messages are still generated and transmitted.

123 is called ALL NOTES OFF, and has the function of stopping all sound being generated from an instrument. However, as NOTE

ON and NOTE OFF commands are usually paired, interrupting the sound is contrary to normal practice, so in general the ALL NOTES OFF command is ignored. Originally ALL NOTES OFF was created to cope with situations where erroneous NOTE ON messages were received. This turned NOTE ON messages into NOTE OFF.

Also some keyboards implement an automatic ALL NOTES OFF function when you remove your fingers from the keys. So with such a keyboard as your master instrument the slaves stop sounding when you stop playing. ALL NOTES OFF has many different uses but is not universally supported and the other Mode messages can be used to achieve similar effects.

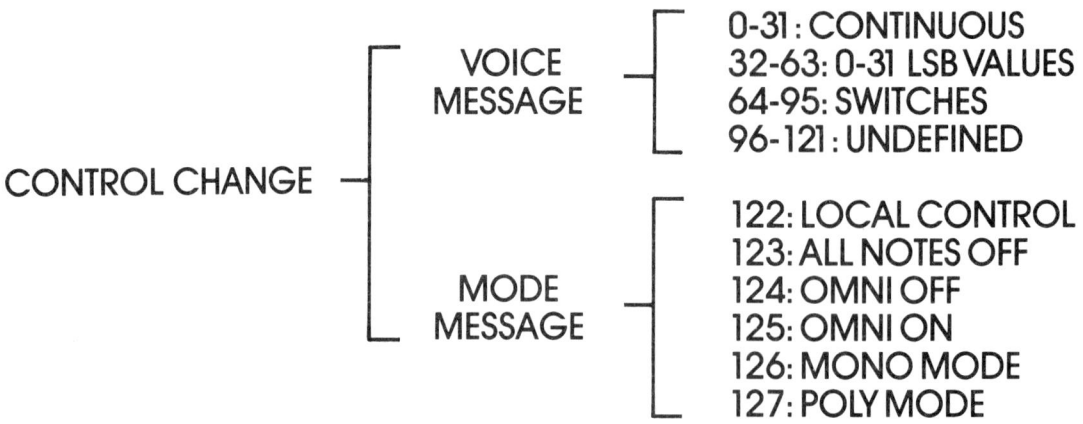

Fig. 45

SOFTWARE: THE PITCH WHEEL
Why It Has Its Own MIDI Message

If you look at the PITCH WHEEL you might think that it has a CONTROL CHANGE message, but in fact it has its own independent MIDI message. The Pitch Wheel is an essential controller for a synthesiser and pitch wheel data is frequently used just like the NOTE ON/OFF events. Another consideration is that CONTROL CHANGE has no function which acts like the Pitch Wheel in being "hyperbolic" – that is moving both up and down about a central null point (0).

Very often beginners make the mistake of trying to use the Pitch bender and getting no result because they fail to realise that usually the degree of pitch bend can be separately set on their instrument, and that if it is set to a value of zero then they generate no effect. However the PITCH WHEEL message is sent independently of the setting of the pitch bend range. The extent of this range depends on how your particular slave instrument has been set up. If you just connect the master to the slave, very often the degree of pitch bend on both instruments is very different, so you have to make sure that they are correctly co-ordinated, usually to an equal range. Another point is that different manufacturers use different degrees (or curves) of pitch bend, sometimes only the start and end points having the same pitch, so a lot of experimentation is necessary for you to become familiar with the many possible combinations available.

Not only PITCH WHEEL but also CONTROL CHANGE messages can have different effects because of the unique ways of setting these parameters on a particular instrument. Very often a function is available to cancel these effects by using a 'MIDI Switch'. If you activate an effect and then the MIDI cable becomes disengaged, the pitch may continue to be shifted, or the sound may play continuously because the damper has been held on. In general these mishaps don't happen that often, but when you stop a sequencer in the middle of autoplay for example problems are much more likely to occur.

HARDWARE

The PITCH WHEEL MIDI message consists of the status byte EnH and 2 data bytes. Each data byte has a range of 128 values (0-127), but the degree of resolution possible using a single data byte is too coarse to achieve smooth pitch sliding, so that it is necessary to utilise two data bytes to express the degree of pitch bend. Two bytes – yes, but as bit 7 of a data byte is set to 0 (to indicate that it is a data byte) we are left with a 14 bit resolution, this however still gives a range of values of 16,384 – a greatly improved accuracy. (See Fig.46)

When you send 2-byte data using CONTROL CHANGE you have to divide the message into two parts, which slows down the response time, so from the point of view of accuracy it seems natural to give Pitch Wheel information (which requires 2-byte

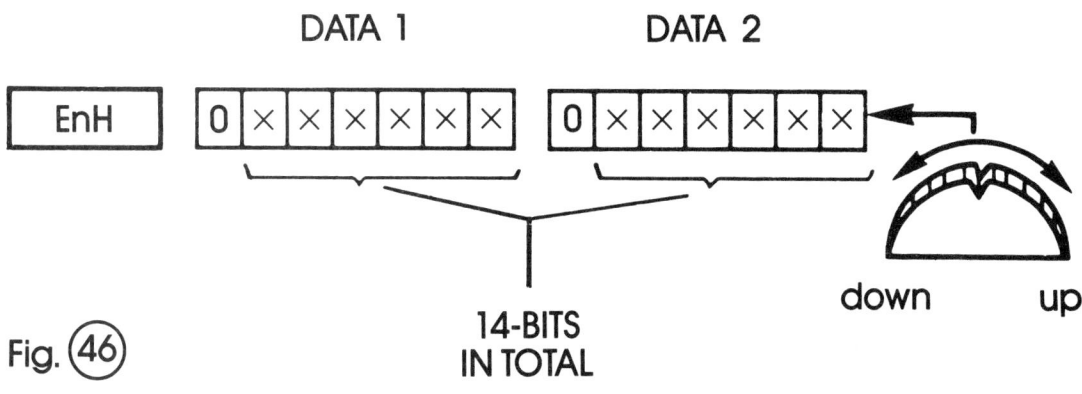

Fig. 46

resolution) its own separate status byte. However there are as yet few synthesisers which provide 14-bit accuracy, most pitch wheels provide only 8-10 bit resolution.

SOFTWARE: SYSTEM MESSAGES
Information Used By The Whole System

When you think about a MIDI system, for example in the case of automatic play, you have to consider control of the whole system including the synchronisation of sequencer and rhythm machines. Channel MIDI messages are MIDI data which control each particular instrument using normal play information. As well as these Channel messages MIDI also includes other commands called System messages which apply to the whole system with no distinction between MIDI channels (see Fig.48). System messages come in three forms;

SYSTEM EXCLUSIVE MESSAGE: which is not standardised, being different for each manufacturer's instruments and is used for exchanging data like voice parameters, drum pattern edit or voice edit when using computers. This allows more possibilities to link with more sophisticated or advanced instruments in the future.

SYSTEM COMMON MESSAGE: which is used to control rhythm machines and sequencers and often used with the Real Time Message.

MIDI SYSTEM

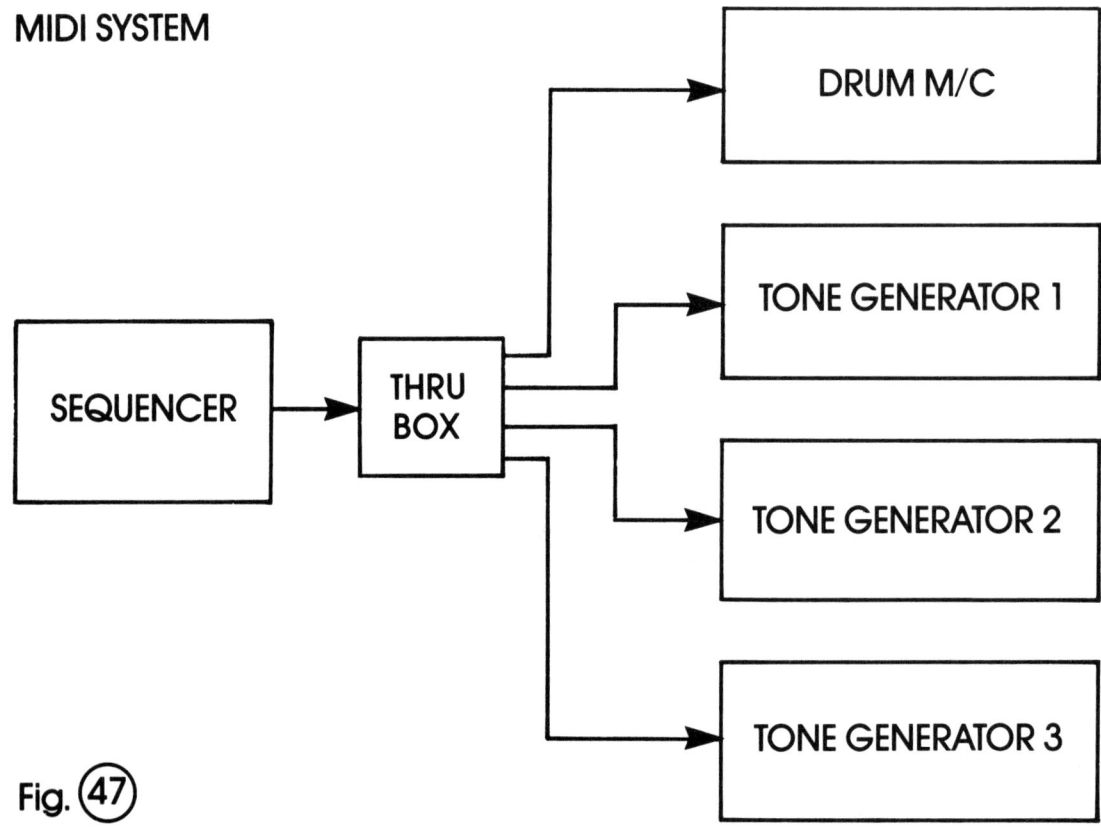

Fig. (47)

MIDI BASICS

SYSTEM REAL TIME MESSAGE: which co-ordinates the whole system.

The SYSTEM EXCLUSIVE message is impossible to standardise because it exists to facilitate the different hardware and software, structures and concepts of individual manufacturers' instruments. SYSTEM EXCLUSIVE messages therefore expand the ability of MIDI to control in a practical way, the individual features of particular instruments e.g. exchanging voice data between compatible instruments or voice editing, pattern editing on drum machines or voice editing using computer controlled software.

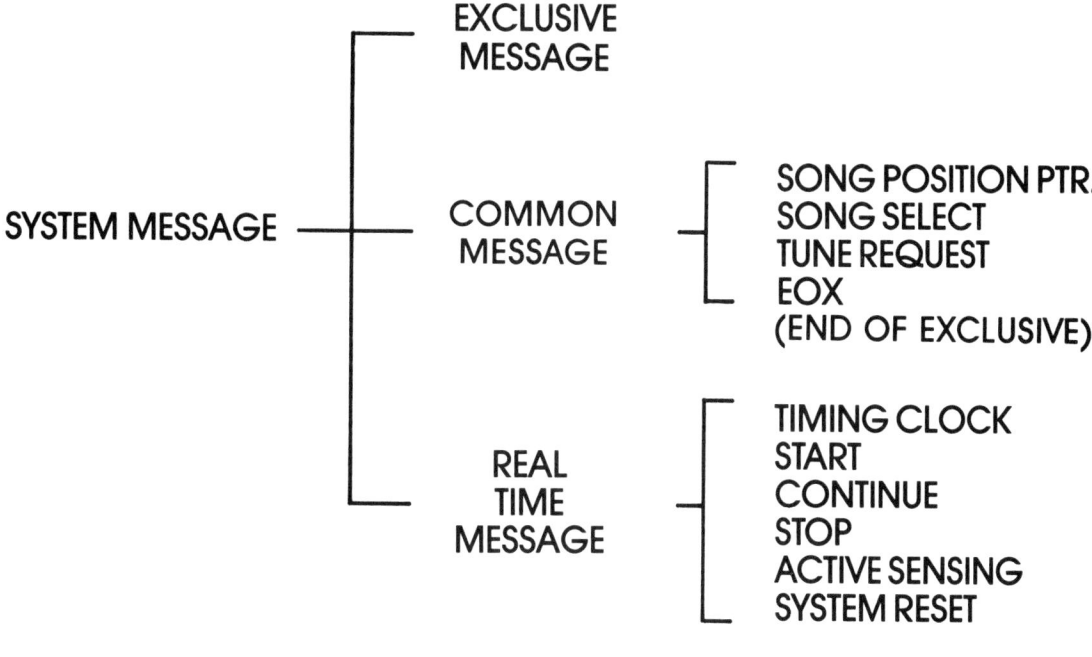

Fig. 48

SYSTEM COMMON and SYSTEM REAL TIME messages are very often used together. If we consider an example of automatic play you will get the idea – first of all you select the number of the particular sequence you wish to play using the SONG SELECT command, and then designate which step of which bar you wish to start playing using the SONG POSITION POINTER (or PTR). Now you will be able to control the autoplay using START/CONTINUE/STOP MIDI commands and synchronisation is achieved using TIMING CLOCK (MIDI CLOCK) commands.

The TUNE REQUEST command instructs analog synthesisers which have an auto-tune function to tune themselves. The END OF EXCLUSIVE message is also included among SYSTEM COMMON messages.

ACTIVE SENSING is used to detect if the MIDI cable has been disconnected, and if so stop all sound being produced. If no other MIDI commands are being sent an ACTIVE SENSING MIDI command (which is called a dummy message because it has no contents) is sent at least every 300mSec. If within 300mS no MIDI message is received then the ACTIVE SENSING switches off all sound generation on the slave instrument. MIDI messages are Asynchronous, so this ACTIVE SENSING was invented to avoid difficulties created by slaves not receiving NOTE OFF messages and playing sounds continuously.

SYSTEM RESET returns the equipment to the state it was in when it was initially turned on. This command is rarely used.

HARDWARE

You can send MIDI SYSTEM EXCLUSIVE messages by placing the necessary data bytes between the two status bytes F 0H and F 7H (END OF EXCLUSIVE: EOX). This MIDI message is the only one which does not use the standard MIDI message format (status byte: data bytes (s)). All manufacturers use their own data format, but the first data byte is called the ID Number and each manufacturer has his own registered ID Number. So if you look at this number you can discover which manufacturer's instrument generated a message (see chart) (Fig.49).

Each SYSTEM EXCLUSIVE message is unique to one manufacturer, and generally includes large amounts of data – synthesiser voice parameters, sequence data etc., consequently exchanging this type of MIDI data can use up quite a lot of time. In general SYSTEM EXCLUSIVE MIDI messages are not received or transmitted, but can be turned on using a separate control switch; so to use MIDI SYSTEM EXCLUSIVE commands you must make certain that this is switched to ON.

ID NO. CHART
1H   SEQUENTIAL CIRCUITS
4H   MOOG
5H   PASSPORT DESIGNS
6H   LEXICON
7H   KURZWEIL
10H OBERHEIM
40H KAWAI
41H ROLAND
42H KORG
43H YAMAHA

Fig.

MIDI BASICS

THE SYSTEM EXCLUSIVE MESSAGE

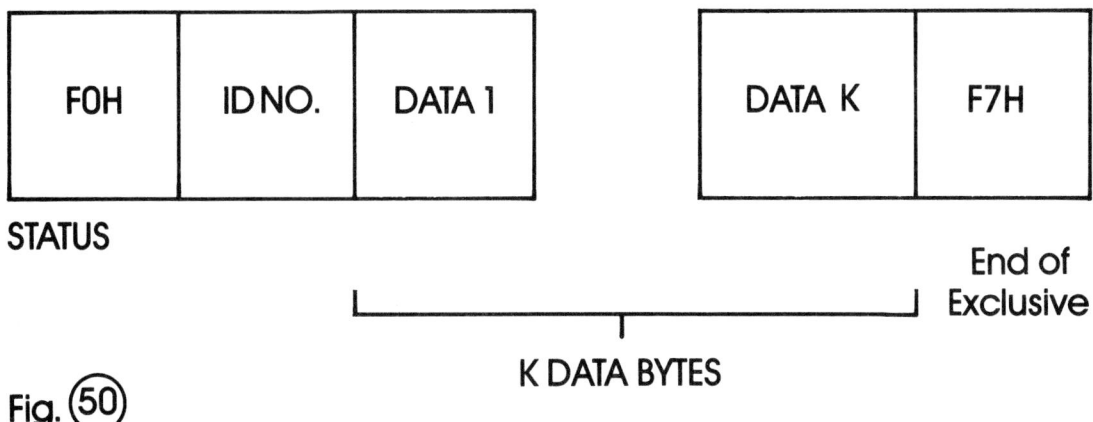

Fig. 50

SYSTEM REAL TIME messages as the name implies control system timing precisely. They have priority over other MIDI messages, so that often these messages take precedence over other MIDI messages being transmitted. MIDI CLOCK status byte F8H is a synchronising timebase of ♩=24 (24-ppqn; pulses per quarter note), meaning that F8H is sent 24 times every quarter note. Remember that in order to achieve synchronised play you have to put the slave instrument into the 'MIDI SYNC' mode.

The functions of FAH (START), FBH (CONTINUE) and FCH (STOP) are self-explanatory, if you press a Start/Cont/Stop button on a rhythm machine immediately the appropriate MIDI commands are sent. FAH/FBH/FCH have no timing function by themselves, if for

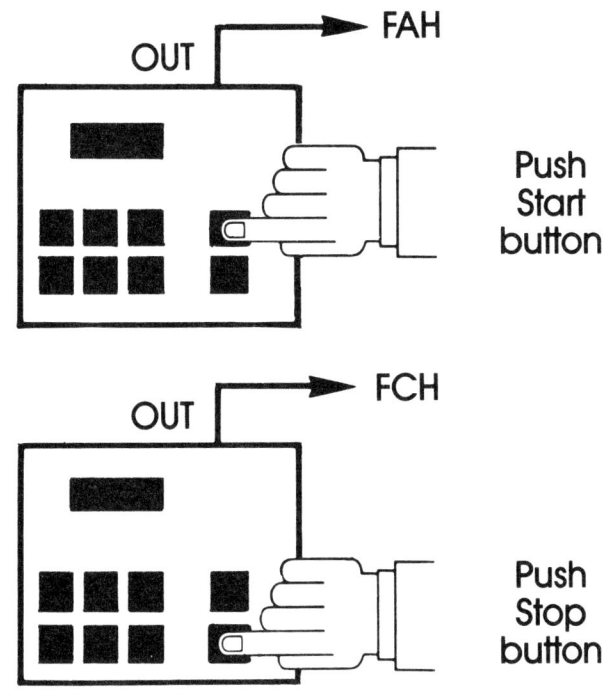

Fig. 51

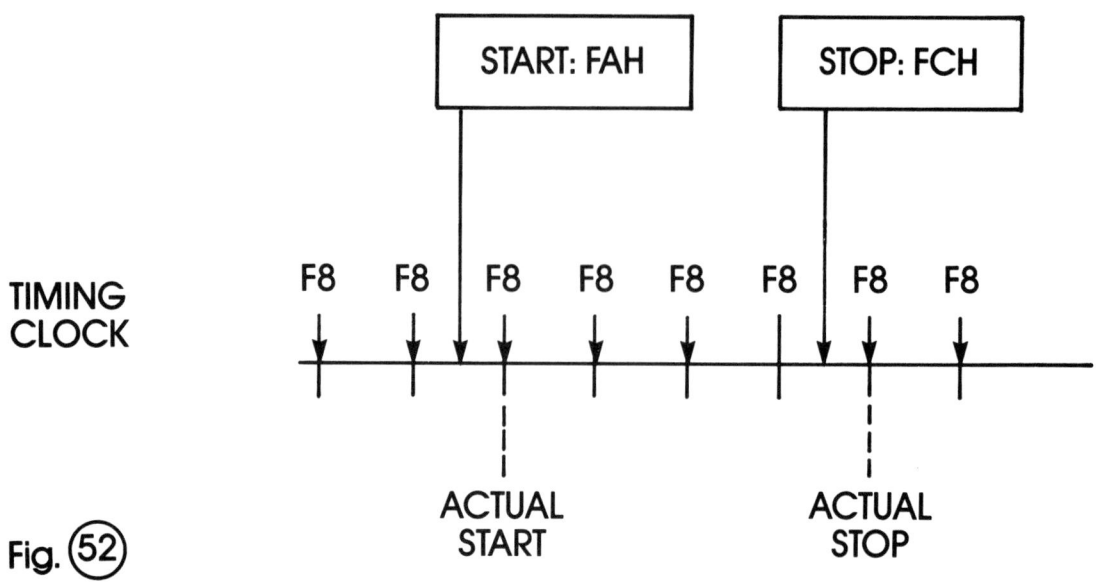

Fig. 52

example we send a START command FAH the machine will start to play after the next clock command F8H is received. SYSTEM REAL TIME messages do not interfere with RUNNING STATUS messages so that it is not necessary to 'keep' the status byte when you program data into the appropriate software.

As MIDI SYSTEM COMMON messages need a certain amount of time to be digested, in the case of automatic play it is best to avoid sending SYSTEM REAL TIME messages immediately after SYSTEM COMMON messages. The SONG SELECT command consists of a status byte F3H followed by a data byte containing the Song Select Number enabling you to choose between previously recorded sequences stored in your machine's memory if it supports this MIDI function. Also the SONG POSITION PTR identifies a precise position within a song by giving the MIDI Beat Number – expressed in two data bytes following the status byte F2H. One MIDI Beat is equal to 6 MIDI Clocks.

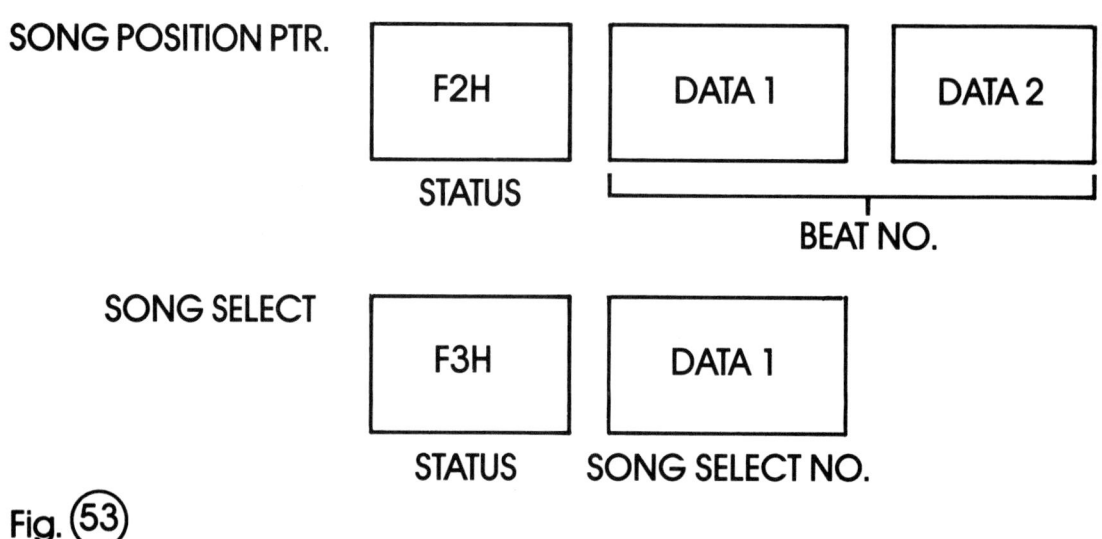

Fig. 53

IMPLEMENTATION CHART

When you connect up MIDI instruments you first have to know how each instrument utilises the MIDI format. The MIDI Implementation Chart, which conforms to the standards drawn up at the original MIDI manufacturers' conference, shows how the instruments utilise the format. With a unified format it is easy to judge the degree of compatibility in MIDI communications, and by comparing the implementation charts provided for each instrument you can easily understand the different MIDI commands and the manner in which they operate. The charts have been organised so that transmission and reception formats can be compared for each instrument by folding (copies of) both charts along the central dividing line and placing them together. If the corresponding rows of both charts contain a "0", then instruments can communicate within the limits of their hardware.

At the head of each chart is a description of the type of instrument in parentheses, and underneath are the model and version numbers. "Transmitted" means commands sent via the MIDI OUT socket, while "Recognised" means commands received. According to the type of instrument, the MIDI input/output modes are controlled by switches and are called instrument modes I/II/III or 1/2/3 etc. In the Yamaha chart '*' also indicates such modes. If there is a correspondence in the row relating to a command, you will find a "0" or the limiting value; if not, there will be an "X". The term "Default" refers to the condition of power up, while "memorised" means that the value of the commands operative at the time the power was cut has been memorised.

"Channel changed" indicates the range of MIDI channels that can be user-defined (e.g. 1-16) For example, when the Basic Default value in the Transmitted column is 1 and Channel changed is X then the MIDI output is restricted to channel 1.

"Modes" are indicated by the number 1-4: 1 = OMNI ON/POLY, 2 = OMNI ON/MONO, 3 = OMNI OFF/POLY, and 4 = OMNI OFF/MONO. "Messages" shows the modes that can be sent and received while "Altered" shows the change in mode when the mode messages are received.

"Note number" indicates the pitch of notes sent and received. If the range is from 1 to 127 (where D is Note Off) then that covers the whole possible range available for MIDI transmissions, but even though 1-127 is shown as available for reception, what is actually

MIDI BASICS

voiced is generally within a narrower range, but it is still recognised and voiced in the correct pitch order. The actual range is shown as "True voice".

"Velocity" has a range of values from 1-127 and a default value of 64 indicating Velocity OFF. If Note Off is represented by the status byte 90H then Velocity = the fixed value of 0. In the key's After Touch (i.e. Poly Pressure) and Ch's After Touch (i.e. Channel Pressure) rows, you will find the values "0" or "X". The same applies to the Pitch Wheel together with any necessary data for its range of resolution.

In the case of "Control Change" as well as 0/X and the Control Number, you will find in the "Remarks" column the name of the appropriate control device. 0 and X also appear in the "System Exclusive" row and you will find further explanation in the "Remarks" column. "System Common" is divided into "Song Pos" "Song Sel" and "Tune" (i.e. Tune Request).

The "System Real Time" row is divided into "Clock" (the master MIDI Clock) and "Commands" (Start/Continue/Stop).

"Aux Message" indicates the auxiliary commands: LOCAL ON/OFF, ALL NOTES OFF (and the corresponding data values for this command, which are greater than 123), ACTIVE SENSING and RESET.

MIDI SPECIFICATIONS: DESCRIPTION

		STATUS BYTE	NO. OF DATA BYTES	DATA		
		MSB LSB		DATA BYTE 1	DATA BYTE 2	
CHANNEL MESSAGE / VOICE MESSAGE	NOTE OFF	8XH `1 0 0 0 X X X X`	2	0~127 (Pitch Number)	0~127 (VELOCITY)	"KEY RELEASE" info (8 XH: STATUS Byte or 9XH, with velocity = 0)
	NOTE ON	9XH `1 0 0 1 X X X X`	2	0 12 24 36 48 60 72 84 96 108 120 127 $\quad G^8$ $C^{-1} C^{-2} C^0 C^1 C^2 C^3 C^4 C^5 C^6 C^7 C^8$	0 1~127 (VELOCITY)	"PRESS KEY" info
	POLY PRESSURE	AXH `1 0 1 0 X X X X`	2		0~127 (PRESSURE)	INDEPENDENT KEY AFTER TOUCH INFO.
	CONTROL CHANGE	BXH `1 0 1 1 X X X X` LSB INDICATES THE MIDI CHANNEL `X X X X` 0 0 0 0 : ch 1 (0 H) 0 0 0 1 : ch 2 (1 H) 0 0 1 0 : ch 3 (2 H) 0 0 1 1 : ch 4 (3 H) 0 1 0 0 : ch 5 (4 H) 0 1 0 1 : ch 6 (5 H) 0 1 1 0 : ch 7 (6 H) 0 1 1 1 : ch 8 (7 H) 1 0 0 0 : ch 9 (8 H) 1 0 0 1 : ch10 (9 H) 1 0 1 0 : ch11 (A H) 1 0 1 1 : ch12 (B H) 1 1 0 0 : ch13 (C H) 1 1 0 1 : ch14 (D H) 1 1 1 0 : ch15 (E H) 1 1 1 1 : ch16 (F H)	2	0 UNDEFINED 1 MODULATION WHEEL OR LEVER 2 BREATH CONTROLLER 3 AFTER TOUCH 4 FOOT CONTROLLER 5 PORTAMENTO TIME 6 DATA ENTRY 7 MAIN VOLUME 8 ~ 31 UNDEFINED 32 ~ 63 LSB of 0 - 31 64 DAMPER PEDAL (SUSTAIN) 65 PORTAMENTO 66 SOSTENUTO 67 SOFT PEDAL 68~92 UNDEFINED 93 CHORUS 94 CELESTE 95 PHASER 96 DATA ENTRY +1 97 DATA ENTRY −1 98~121 UNDEFINED	0~127 (MSB) 0~127 LSB 0 : OFF 127 : ON	CONTROL INFO. OF EFFECTS UNITS 0~31: CONTINUOUS CONTROLLERS (LEVER PEDALS ETC.) 32~63: WHEN GREATER ACCURACY IS REQUIRED, THESE ARE USED AS THE LSB OF 0-31 64~95 SWITCHES 96~121 USER-DEFINED

MIDI BASICS

MODE MESSAGES				122 LOCAL CONTROL	0: OFF 127: ON	THE COMMAND TO CUT OFF KEYBOARD AND SOUND GENERATION.
				123 ALL NOTES OFF	0	THE COMMAND TO DISABLE THE INSTRUMENT.
				124 OMNI MODE OFF 125 OMNI MODE ON 126 MONO ON/POLY OFF 127 POLY ON/MONO OFF	0 0 0~15 (M) 0	RECOGNISES THE CHANNEL DOES NOT RECOGNISE CHANNEL SINGLE VOICE PER CHANNEL ALL VOICES IN A SINGLE CHANNEL } The 4 Modes
	VOICE MESSAGE	PROGRAM CHANGE	CXH [1][1][1][0][0][X][X][X] 1	0~127 PROGRAM NUMBER		INFO. ABOUT WHEN A TIMER SELECT KEY IS PUSHED.
		CHANNEL PRESSURE	DXH [1][1][0][1][X][X][X][X] 1	0~127 (PRESSURE)		AFTER TOUCH INFO. ABOUT THE WHOLE INSTRUMENT.
		PITCH WHEEL	EXH [1][1][1][0][X][X][X][X] 2	0~127 LSB	0~127 (MSB)	INFO ON PITCH WHEEL OPERATION.
SYSTEM MESSAGE	SYSTEM EXCLUSIVE		F0H [1][1][1][1][0][0][0][0] ANY	0~127 (I D CODE)	ANY No. of DATA BYTES	MANUFACTURERS INDIVIDUALLY REGISTERED I D. CODE.
		UNDEFINED	F1H			
	SYSTEM COMMON	SONG POSITION	F2H [1][1][1][1][0][0][1][0] 2	0~127 LSB	0~127 (MSB)	START OF THE SONG IN MIDI BITS (1 MIDI BIT = 6 MIDI CLOCKS).
		SONG SELECT	F3H [1][1][1][1][0][0][1][1] 1	0~127 SONG NUMBER		RHYTHM MACHINE: BANK SELECT
		UNDEFINED	F4H~F5H			
		TUNE REQUEST	F6H [1][1][1][1][0][1][1][0] 0			THE COMMAND FOR ANALOGUE SYNTHESISERS TO AUTO TUNE
		END OF EXCLUSIVE	F7H [1][1][1][1][0][1][0][1] 0			INDICATES THE END OF THE SYSTEM EXCLUSIVE COMMAND
	SYSTEM REAL TIME	TIMING CLOCK	F8H [1][1][1][1][1][0][0][0] 0			MIDI MASTER CLOCK (♩ = 24) TIME BASE
		UNDEFINED	F9H			
		START	FAH [1][1][1][1][1][0][1][0] 0			APPLIES TO START/CONTINUE/STOP ON SEQUENCERS (et al.)
		CONTINUE	FBH [1][1][1][1][1][0][1][1] 0			
		STOP	FCH [1][1][1][1][1][1][0][0] 0			
		UNDEFINED	FDH			
		ACTIVE SENSING	FEH [1][1][1][1][1][1][1][0] 0			COMMAND SENT EVERY 300m SECS. TO PREVENT PROBLEMS CAUSED BY DISCONNECTION OF MIDI CABLE
		SYSTEM RESET	FFH [1][1][1][1][1][1][1][1] 0			INITIALISES BACK TO THE CONDITION AT POWER UP.

INDEX

Active Sensing	32, 49
Aftertouch	39, 40
Analog Synth	29
Baud Rate	27
Bit	30
Byte	30, 31
Channel Information	14, 17, 18, 19, 37
Channel Pressure	41
Computer	28
Control Change	37, 47
Control Number	44
C/V Gate Control	28, 29
D/A Conversion	23, 24
Data Channels	11
DIN MIDI Cable	5, 25
Drum Machines/Rhythm Machines	13, 20, 25, 43
Guitar synth	20
LSB	31
MIDI Cable Connection	5, 6, 25, 32
MIDI Cable Length	26
MIDI Channels	10, 33, 36
MIDI Characters	27
MIDI Circuits	27
MIDI Clock	43, 49
MIDI Compatible	20
MIDI Data	17
MIDI Delay	7, 8, 22
MIDI Expansion/Thru Box	8, 9, 13, 23
MIDI Message	27, 28
MIDI Modes	14, 36-39
MIDI Note Numbers	35
MIDI Specification	18, 27
MIDI Terminals	6, 21, 22, 24
Mixers	20
Modulation Wheel	17
MSB	31
Note Number	31
Phototransistor	24
Pitch Bender	20
Pitch Wheel	30, 46, 47
Polyphonic Key Pressure	41
Portamento	17
Pressure	31
Program Change	18, 41, 42
Pulse Wave	27
Running Status	34
Sequencers	13, 25, 28
Song Position Ptr.	49, 52
Song Select	49
Status Byte	34
System Information	18, 19
System Messages	48, 49
Tone Generators	20, 45
Touch Sensitivity	18, 35
Transpose	33
Tremolo	39
UART	24
Velocity	31, 33, 35
Vibrato	39
Voltage Control	29

Other Technical Books for Musicians.

The Complete Synthesizer.
By David Crombie.
Tells you all you need to know about synthesizers, the way they work and how to get the best out of them. In clear text, backed up with diagrams, this book deals with The Three Elements of Sound, Standard Tuning, Frequency & Music, Types of Synthesizer, Voltage Control, The Filter, Accessories and other related subjects.

Omnibus Press
104 pages
Order No. OP 41649
ISBN 0.7119.0056.6

The New Complete Synthesizer.
By David Crombie.
All aspects of electronic music are explained with clear text and diagrams – both for the newcomer and the experienced synthesist.

Omnibus Press
104 pages
Order No. OP 43421
ISBN 0.7119.0701.3

Home Recording for Musicians.
By Craig Anderton.
Making a demo tape or an independent single, this book will provide an in-depth guide right from basic recording equipment to mixing and mastering techniques. Save yourself hours of studio time!

Amsco Publications
184 pages
Order No. AM 32699
ISBN 0.7119.0214.3

The Digital Delay Handbook.
By Craig Anderton.
Whether live or in the studio, this handbook helps you to create a signal processing magic with one of the most popular and commonly available effects. Some of the topics covered are Short Delay Applications, Automatic Flanging, Phase Shifter Simulation, Robot Voices, Reverb Pre-delay, and Synchro-Sonic Echo Effects.

Amsco Publications
132 pages
Order No. AM 38985
ISBN 0.8256.2414.2

The Complete Guide to Synthesizers, Sequencers & Drum Machines.
By Dean Friedman.
A guide to the purchasing of an instrument. Organised in order of suggested retail price, this book is profusely illustrated with the latest devices along with technical specifications.

Amsco Publications
112 pages
Order No. AM 38688
ISBN 0.8256.2414.2

Yamaha DX7 Digital Synthesizer.
By Yasuhiko Fukuda.
All you need to know to successfully operate the DX7. Describes procedures for editing, tone creation, and advanced sound making techniques – as well as the basic mechanism.

Amsco Publications
144 pages
Order No. AM 39371
ISBN 0.7119.0653.X

MIDI for Musicians.
By Craig Anderton.
The revolutionary concept of MIDI will affect the way we play, record, compose and even transcribe music – this book explains why in clear text and diagrams. Some of the topics covered are the MIDI language and what it means in musical terms, MIDI applications live and in the studio, musician-orientated software and accessories, and how computers work in musical applications.

Amsco Publications
120 pages
Order No. AM 61219
ISBN 0.7119.0822.2

Electronic Projects for Musicians.
By Craig Anderton.
How to build your own Preamp, Compressor/Limiter, Ring Modulator, Phase Shifter, and Talk Box – plus 22 other inexpensive accessories – all described in easy-to-follow language backed by hundreds of diagrams.

Amsco Publications
224 pages
Order No. AM 32707
ISBN 0.7119.0270.4

Guitar Electronics for Musicians.
By Donald Brosnac.
Anyone who wants information on guitar construction and function will benefit from this book. Electronics are clearly explained with over 350 photographs, drawings and schematics. The sound of the electric guitar is followed through. from the vibration of the strings to pick-ups, volume and tone controls, switches, and finally an output jack or cordless transmitter and amplifier.

Omnibus Press
128 pages
Order No. OP 42324
ISBN 0.7119.0232.1

Electronic Drums.
By Frank Vilardi with Steve Tarshis.
The indispensable guide to electronic drum kits and drum computers – what to look for when buying, how they work, and programming procedures. Includes a breakdown of leading brand names, from the earliest Syndrum to the most recent Linn drum computer.

Amsco Publications
96 pages
Order No. AM 37342
ISBN 0.7119.0747.1

Guitar Gadgets.
By Craig Anderton.
A consumer's guide to electronic gadgets for the guitar with advice on buying, applying, and getting the best out of them. Among the subjects dealt with in this important publication are Understanding Specifications, Printed Circuit Board Checks, Input Impedance, Parametric Equalisers, Harmony Synthesising Devices.

Omnibus Press
192 pages
Order No. AM34174
ISBN 0.7119.0392.1

Synthesizer Basics.
By Dean Friedman.
The definitive beginner's guide. Tells you everything you need to know to really understand, program, and start using your synthesizer. Contains special sections on the Yamaha DX7, Sampling Devices and MIDI.
  Over 35 practical exercises, plus a complete glossary of terms.

Amsco Publications
160 pages
Order No. AM 38696
ISBN 0.7119.1022.7

Amsco and Omnibus titles are available from good book and music shops.
In case of difficulty, contact
Book Sales Limited, Newmarket Road, Bury St. Edmunds, Suffolk IP33 3YB.